Ve

DIRECTIONS

WRITTEN AND RESEARCHED BY

Jonathan Buckley

NEW YORK • LONDON • DELHI
www.roughguides.com

Contents

Introduction to

Venice

Founded 1500 years ago on a cluster of mudflats in the centre of the lagoon, Venice rose to become Europe's main trading post between the West and the East, and at its height controlled an empire that extended from the Dolomites to Cyprus. The melancholic air of the place is in part a product of the discrepancy between the grandeur of its history and what the city has become.

The Záttere, Dorsoduro

In the heyday of the Venetian Republic, some 200,000 people lived in Venice, three times its present population. Merchants from Europe and western Asia maintained warehouses here; transactions in the banks and bazaars of the Rialto dictated the value of commodities all over the continent; in the dockyards of the Arsenale

▲ Gondola, under the Rialto bridge

When to visit

Venice's tourist season is very nearly an all-year affair. Peak season, when hotel rooms are virtually impossible to come by at short notice, is from **April to October**; try to avoid **July and August** in particular, when the climate becomes oppressively hot and clammy. The other two popular spells are the **Carnevale** (leading up to Lent) and the weeks on each side of **Christmas**.

For the ideal combination of comparative peace and a mild climate, the two or three weeks **immediately preceding Easter** is perhaps the best time of year. Climatically the months at the end of the high season are somewhat less reliable: some **November and December** days bring fogs that make it difficult to see from one bank of the Canal Grande to the other. If you want to see the city at its quietest, **January** is the month to go – take plenty of warm clothes, though, as the winds off the Adriatic can be savage, and you should be prepared for floods throughout the winter. This **acqua alta**, as Venice's seasonal flooding is called, has been an element of Venetian life for centuries, but nowadays it's far more frequent than it used to be: between October and late February it's not uncommon for flooding to occur every day of the week, and it'll be a long time before the huge flood barrier (which was begun in 2003) makes any impact. However, having lived with it for so long, the city is well geared to dealing with the nuisance. Shopkeepers in the most badly affected areas insert steel shutters into their doorways to hold the water at bay, while the local council lays jetties of duck-boards along the major thoroughfares and between the chief vaporetto stops and dry land.

the workforce was so vast that a warship could be built and fitted out in a single day; and the Piazza San Marco was thronged with people here to set up deals or report to the Republic's government. Nowadays it's no longer a buzzing metropolis but rather the embodiment of a fabulous past, dependent for its survival largely on the people who come to marvel at its relics.

The monuments which draw the largest crowds are the Basilica di San Marco – the mausoleum of the city's patron saint – and the Palazzo Ducale or Doge's Palace. Certainly these are the most imposing structures in the city, but a roll-call of the churches worth visiting would feature more than a dozen names. Many of the city's treasures remain in the churches for which they were created, but a sizeable number have

◀ Al Ponte osteria, Cannaregio

▲ Rio di San Trovaso, Dorsoduro

been removed to one or other of Venice's museums, with the Accademia holding the lion's share. This cultural heritage is a source of endless fascination, but you should also discard your itineraries for a day and just wander – the anonymous parts of Venice reveal as much of the city as its well-known attractions.

The historic centre of Venice is made up of 118 islands, tied together by some four hundred bridges to form an amalgamation that's divided into six large administrative districts known as *sestieri*, three on each side of the Canal Grande.

◄ The Mercerie area

Venice
AT A GLANCE

SAN MARCO

The *sestiere* of San Marco is the hub of the city, being the location of the two prime monuments – the Palazzo Ducale and the Basilica di San Marco – and the city's highest concentration of shops and hotels.

San Barnaba, Dorsoduro

▲ The Basilica and Palazzo Ducale

CASTELLO

Spreading north and east of San Marco, the sprawling *sestiere* of Castello encompasses many of Venice's most interesting churches, its former industrial centre and some of its grittier residential areas.

DORSODURO

Lying on the opposite side of the Canal Grande from San Marco, and stretching westward to the docks, Dorsoduro is one of the city's smartest quarters, as well as the home of its university and the main art gallery.

San Zanipolo, Castello

◄ Campo San Polo

SAN POLO AND SANTA CROCE

Adjoining Dorsoduro to the north, the *sestieri* of San Polo and Santa Croce are riddled with intricate alleyways and characterful little squares – and it's here that you'll find the famous Rialto market.

◄ San Michele, northern islands

NORTHERN ISLANDS

The nearest of the northern islands of the lagoon – San Michele – is the city's historic cemetery; a little farther out lies the glassmaking island of Murano, while in the outermost reaches you'll find Burano and Torcello, Venice's predecessor.

SOUTHERN ISLANDS

Sheltered from the Adriatic by the Lido and its neighbouring sandbanks, the southern part of the lagoon has a scattering of islands, notably San Giorgio Maggiore and La Giudecca, the focus of some major redevelopment projects.

▲ Fondamenta di Cannaregio

CANNAREGIO

The train station occupies a corner of Cannaregio, and most of the city's one-star hotels are clustered nearby, but much of this district is tranquil and unaffected by the influx of tourists.

▲ San Giorgio Maggiore, southern islands

Ideas

The big six

In effect all of central Venice is one vast and astounding sight, and you'd have a great time if you were to spend your days here just wandering at random. That said, there are some specific monuments and museums you really should make a point of visiting. Here are six of Venice's foremost attractions, each one of them amazing.

▲ The Scuola Grande di San Rocco

Rome has the Sistine Chapel, Florence has the Brancacci Chapel, and Venice has the Scuola Grande di San Rocco, with its overwhelming cycle of paintings by Jacopo Tintoretto.

P.101 ▸ SAN POLO AND SANTA CROCE

▼ The Frari

The gargantuan edifice of Santa Maria Gloriosa dei Frari contains masterpieces by Titian, Bellini, Donatello and many more.

P.99 ▸ SAN POLO AND SANTA CROCE

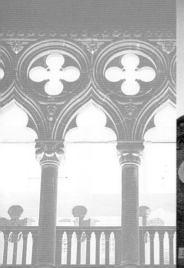

▶ Santi Giovanni e Paolo

The vast Dominican church of Santi Giovanni e Paolo is the mausoleum of the doges, containing some of the city's finest sculpture.

P.118 ▸ CENTRAL CASTELLO

◀ The Accademia

In the Accademia's magnificent galleries you can trace the development of painting in Venice from the fifteenth century to the eighteenth, the last golden age of Venetian art.

P.78 ▸ DORSODURO

▼ The Palazzo Ducale

The home of the doges was the nerve-centre of the entire Venetian empire, and was decorated by some of the greatest Venetian artists.

P.54 ▸ SAN MARCO: THE PIAZZA

▼ San Marco

The mosaic-encrusted church of St Mark is the most opulent cathedral in all of Europe.

P.51 ▸ SAN MARCO: THE PIAZZA

The main islands

To get a fuller picture of the Venetian way of life (and death), and an insight into the development of the city, you should make an expedition to some of the outlying islands of the lagoon, where the incursions of the tourist industry are on the whole less obtrusive.

▲ Burano

The brightly painted exteriors of the houses of Burano give this island an appearance that's distinct from any other settlement in the lagoon

P.145 ▸ THE NORTHERN ISLANDS

▼ La Giudecca

Once one of the city's main industrial zones, La Giudecca is nowadays a predominantly residential area that retains much of the spirit of the city prior to the age of mass tourism.

P.151 ▸ THE SOUTHERN ISLANDS

▶ San Michele

Located a short distance north of the city centre, San Michele is possibly the most beautiful cemetery in the world.

P.142 ▶ THE NORTHERN ISLANDS

▼ Murano

Glass has been the basis of Murano's economy for seven hundred years, and there are still plenty of factories where you can admire the glassblowers' amazing skills.

P.143 ▶ THE NORTHERN ISLANDS

▼ Torcello

The majestic cathedral of Torcello – the oldest building in the whole lagoon – marks the spot where the lagoon city came into existence.

P.147 ▶ THE NORTHERN ISLANDS

Museums and art galleries

The Accademia packs a bigger punch than any of Venice's other museums, so if you have time for only one collection the choice is pretty straightforward. But it would be a shame not to sample some of the more specialized museums, which cover everything from the maritime and political history of the republic to the art of the twentieth century.

▼ The Guggenheim

For a break from the Renaissance, spend an hour or two with the Guggenheim's fine array of modern art.

P.80 ▶ DORSODURO

▼ Ca' d'Oro

Once the most extravagant house on the Canal Grande, the Ca' d'Oro today is home to an engagingly miscellaneous art collection.

P.113 ▶ CANNAREGIO

◀ Museo Storico Navale

As you'd expect from a city whose wealth and power were founded on shipping, the naval museum offers a comprehensive overview of maritime history and technology.

P.130 ▸ EASTERN CASTELLO

▲ Ca' Rezzonico

Devoted to the visual and applied arts of the eighteenth century, the Ca' Rezzonico contains several wonderful paintings and some frankly bizarre furniture.

P.87 ▸ DORSODURO

◀ Museo Correr

Now joined to the Libreria Sansoviniana and the archeological museum, the Correr is a museum of Venetian history with an excellent art gallery upstairs.

P.59 ▸ SAN MARCO: THE PIAZZA

Hotels

As you'd expect in a city that for decades has been one of the world's most popular tourist destinations, Venice is replete with hotels, ranging from eye-poppingly luxurious and expensive palaces to back-alley one-stars with bedrooms barely bigger than a suitcase. Between these two extremes you'll find several places that are both well priced and characterful, and a few that will tempt you to reach for the credit card and damn the consequences.

▲ Bernardi Semenzato

Well located and always hospitable, this simple two-star has long been a favourite of cost-conscious visitors.

P.164 ▶ ACCOMMODATION

▲ Ca' Pisani

At the four-star *Ca' Pisani* the rooms are big and the look of the place harks back to the early-middle years of the twentieth century.

P.163 ▶ ACCOMMODATION

▼ Accademia Villa Maravege

Watch the passing traffic on the Canal Grande as you relax in the garden of this former diplomatic residence.

P.163 ▶ ACCOMMODATION

▲ San Cassiano-Ca' Favretto

A Canal Grande address where the prices won't set you reeling – and the Rialto market is a two-minute stroll away.

P.164 ▶ ACCOMMODATION

▶ Novecento

In a city where brocade and Murano chandeliers are the preferred hotel style, the Eastern-inflected decor of *Novecento* is a highly welcome touch of idiosyncrasy.

P.163 ▶ ACCOMMODATION

▼ La Residenza

It's close to the Piazza, it's in a beautiful old palazzo and it's inexpensive – in Venetian terms, anyway.

P.166 ▶ ACCOMMODATION

Venice viewpoints

Venice is the most photogenic of cities, and wherever you're standing you'll see something memorable. For great panoramic views of the place, however, you should make a beeline for one or more of these vantage points.

▲ Campanile di San Marco

The cathedral's belltower – the tallest structure for miles around – affords grandstand views of the historic centre.

P.57 ▸ SAN MARCO: THE PIAZZA

◀ The Riva

Stretching from the Palazzo Ducale to the Arsenale, the Riva degli Schiavoni is Venice's finest promenade – an unforgettable experience at sunset.

P.123 ▸ CENTRAL CASTELLO

▲ The boat to Burano

For a long-range perspective on the whole of the city, take a trip on the #LN vaporetto from Fondamente Nove out to Burano.

P.142 ▸ THE NORTHERN ISLANDS

▼ San Giorgio Maggiore

The one thing you can't see from the Campanile di San Marco is the Campanile di San Marco and the Riva degli Schiavoni, which is why the best of all lookout towers is the belltower of San Giorgio Maggiore, across the water.

P.150 ▸ THE SOUTHERN ISLANDS

▲ The Záttere

The southern waterfront of Dorsoduro, formerly a busy dock, is nowadays a perfect place for an unhurried stroll and café-stoP.

P.82 ▸ DORSODURO

Palaces

Huge and handsome *palazzi* are to be seen all over Venice, as nearly every parish – in other words, every small island – had its pre-eminent family, and each of these families had its own *palazzo*. Because it cuts through so many parishes, and offers more opportunities for display than any other waterway, the Canal Grande has the majority of these grandiose houses, which span a period of half a millennium.

▲ **Palazzo Grimani**

It took nearly twenty years to build the Palazzo Grimani, the most intimidating palace on the Canal Grande.

P.137 ▶ THE CANAL GRANDE

▲ **Palazzo Grassi**

Constructed in the late eighteenth century, Palazzo Grassi was the last of the city's great palaces, and is now a first-rank exhibition space.

P.74 ▶ THE CANAL GRANDE

▲ Ca' Fóscari

Home of one of the most famous of all the doges, Ca' Fóscari was described by Ruskin as Venice's noblest example of late Gothic architecture.

P.140 ▸ THE CANAL GRANDE

◀ Palazzo Labia

Built by a ludicrously wealthy Spanish family, Palazzo Labia has a ballroom that's decorated with seductive frescoes by Giambattista Tiepolo.

P.108 ▸ THE CANAL GRANDE

▼ Ca' da Mosto

Dating back to the thirteenth century, this picturesque Canal Grande palazzo is a superb example of the Veneto-Byzantine style.

P.136 ▸ THE CANAL GRANDE

Restaurants

If you make the mistake of eating in one of the restaurants near the Piazza, you might well come away thinking that Venice deserves its reputation as a place where mass tourism has produced monotonous menus, cynical service and slapdash standards in the kitchen. Get out into the quieter zones of the city, though, and the picture changes: Venice has an increasing number of excellent (and not necessarily expensive) restaurants, in which – as you'd expect – fresh fish and seafood predominate.

▲ Alla Fontana

The tiny, homely *Alla Fontana* offers superb traditional seafood at extremely reasonable prices.

P.116 ▸ CANNAREGIO

▼ Corte Sconta

Imaginative cuisine and a friendly atmosphere have made *Corte Sconta* a huge success – reservations are almost obligatory.

P.132 ▸ EASTERN CASTELLO

◀ Mistrà

As you weave your way through the Giudecca boatyard you might think you've taken a wrong turning, but keep going – the well-hidden *Mistrà* is a terrific *trattoria*.

P.157 ▸ SOUTHERN ISLANDS

▼ La Bitta

If you feel you can't look another squid in the face, try *La Bitta*, a terrific small *osteria* where meat rules the menu.

P.90 ▸ DORSODURO

◀ Da Fiore

Ask any Venetian to name the best restaurant in the city and nine times out of ten *Da Fiore* will be the answer.

P.105 ▸ SAN POLO AND SANTA CROCE

▶ Anice Stellato

The modern styling and consistently high standards of *Anice Stellato* have made it one of the new stars of the Venice restaurant scene.

P.116 ▸ CANNAREGIO

Scuole

The religious confraternities known as *scuole* are distinctively Venetian institutions. All of them were formed to provide material and spiritual assistance to their members, but some were considerably wealthier than others, as you can see from the profusion of artworks that embellish the headquarters of the so-called Scuole Grande. The Scuola Grande di San Rocco is the most spectacular of them, but others repay a visit too.

▼ Scuola Grande di San Marco

Now Venice's hospital, the Scuola Grande di San Marco is a masterpiece of the early Renaissance, featuring carvings by Tullio and Antonio Lombardo, two of the major figures of the period.

P.120 ▸ CENTRAL CASTELLO

▼ Scuola di San Giovanni Evangelista

The forecourt of the *scuola* of John the Baptist is one of the most alluring episodes in the Venetian cityscape.

P.103 ▸ SAN POLO AND SANTA CROCE

▲ Scuola Grande dei Carmini

The *scuola* of the Carmelites is notable for yet another bravura ceiling by Giambattista Tiepolo.

P.86 ▸ DORSODURO

◀ Scuola di Battioro e Tiraoro

Looking something like an overgrown cabinet, the tiny *scuola* of Venice's goldsmiths is tucked alongside the church of San Stae, right on the Canal Grande.

P.96 ▸ SAN POLO AND SANTA CROCE

▼ Scuola di San Giorgio degli Schiavoni

The Slavs' *scuola* features on many visitors' lists of favourite places in Venice, on account of Carpaccio's dazzling sequence of paintings in the lower hall.

P.128 ▸ EASTERN CASTELLO

Bars

From old-world drinking dens to designer night-spots, Venice has bars for all tastes, but – more than anywhere else in Italy – the division between bars and restaurants is often difficult to draw. A distinctive aspect of the Venetian social scene is the *bacarò*, which is essentially a bar that serves a range of snacks called *cicheti*, plus sometimes more substantial meals. Conversely, many restaurants (often called *osterie*) are fronted by a bar, which may stay open long after the kitchen has shut.

▲ Centrale

So cool it hurts - put on the Prada jacket and get yourself down to *Centrale*, the hippest bar-restaurant in town.

P.76 ▸ SAN MARCO: WEST OF THE PIAZZA

▲ Al Volto

The Veneto produces more DOC (Denomin-azione di origine controllata) wines than any other region of Italy, and there's nowhere better to sample them than *Al Volto*.

P.69 ▸ SAN MARCO: NORTH OF THE PIAZZA

◄ Paradiso Perduto

Nightlife in Venice is pretty tame, but the buzzing *Paradiso Perduto* has been packing them in for years.

P.117 ▸ CANNAREGIO

▼ Café Noir

Open till the small hours, *Café Noir* is a fixture of the student social scene.

P.91 ▸ DORSODURO

▲ Enoteca Mascareta

You can't go home without trying prosecco, the light, champagne-like wine from the area around Conegliano; drop into *Mascareta* for a glass.

P.126 ▸ CENTRAL CASTELLO

◄ Do Mori

No seats, no tables – just good wine and good snacks. *Do Mori* is one of the last of a dying breed.

P.106 ▸ SAN POLO AND SANTA CROCE

Renaissance art and architecture

From the Bellini family to the triumvirate of Titian, Veronese and Tintoretto, Venice nurtured some of the great figures of Renaissance art. For an overview of this Golden Age your first stop should be the Accademia, but that's only the start – many masterpieces still hang in the churches for which they were painted. As for that era's buildings, Venice has some superb Renaissance palaces, and the churches of locally born Andrea Palladio became a model for architects throughout Europe.

▲ San Sebastiano

The parish church of Paolo Veronese is a treasure-house of pictures by the artist, begun before he had turned 30.

P.84 ▶ DORSODURO

▼ Santa Maria Formosa

A powerful image of St Barbara – a masterpiece by Palma il Vecchio – enhances a chapel in the church of Santa Maria Formosa.

P.121 ▶ CENTRAL CASTELLO

▶ San Giorgio Maggiore

Palladio's famed church of San Giorgio Maggiore is home to a pair of paintings that Tintoretto created specifically for the place where they still hang.

▲ The Libreria Sansoviniana and the Zecca

Standing side by side opposite the Palazzo Ducale, the city library and mint were both created by Jacopo Sansovino, the Republic's principal architect in the early sixteenth century.

▲ San Zaccaria

A large and lustrous altarpiece by Giovanni Bellini is the highlight inside this wonderful building.

▶ San Michele in Isola

Designed by Mauro Codussi, this beguiling little church was one of the first Renaissance buildings in Venice.

Shops and markets

Venice is a small city, with a population of under 70,000 in the historic centre, so it doesn't have shopping streets to compare with those of Milan, Florence or Rome. But many of the big Italian labels have outlets in the Mercerie and to the west of the Piazza, and there are several places where you can buy something uniquely Venetian.

▲ Masks

Carnival masks are made year-round in the city's numerous workshops, and their handiwork is amazingly inventive – MondoNovo is one of the very best.

P.89 ▶ DORSODURO

▲ Paper

Marbled paper is another Venetian speciality, sold through various small outlets, such as the famous Legatoria Piazzesi.

P.75 ▶ SAN MARCO: WEST OF THE PIAZZA

▲ Glass

No trip to Venice would be complete without a visit to the furnaces and shops of Murano.

P.143 ▸ THE NORTHERN ISLANDS

▲ The Mercerie

Running from the Piazza to within a few metres of the Rialto Bridge, the Mercerie are the busiest shopping streets in Venice.

P.63 ▸ SAN MARCO: NORTH OF THE PIAZZA

▼ The Rialto

Once the most celebrated market in Europe, the Rialto is still a thriving operation, offering a fabulous array of fresh food – plus thousands of souvenir T-shirts.

P.104 ▸ SAN POLO AND SANTA CROCE

▼ Lace

Lying beyond Murano in the northern lagoon, Burano too has its specialist handicraft – in this case, exquisite lacework.

P.145 ▸ THE NORTHERN ISLANDS

Cafés, cakes and ice cream

Europe's first coffee house opened in Venice in 1683, and nowadays the city has plenty of high-quality cafés, plus some wonderful *pasticcerie* (cake shops), where elbow-room is especially restricted first thing in the morning, when the citizens pile in for a breakfast coffee and *cornetto* (croissant). You can also stop for a coffee at most of Venice's *gelaterie*, where the ice cream comes in a multitude of luscious flavours.

▲ Marchini

Venetian pastries are as delicious as any in Italy, and none are better than those at the renowned Marchini.

P.68 ▶ SAN MARCO: NORTH OF THE PIAZZA

▼ Florian

The most famous café in all of Italy – just try not to keel over when they give you the bill.

P.61 ▶ SAN MARCO: THE PIAZZA

▶ Rosa Salva

It doesn't have the glamour of *Florian*, but many would argue that *Rosa Salva*'s coffee is every bit as good.

P.125 ▸
CENTRAL
CASTELLO

▼ Nico

Take a slab of praline ice cream, slather it with cream, and you've got a *gianduiotto da passeggio*, the speciality at Nico.

P.89 ▸ DORSODURO

▲ Causin

Sample innovative icy concoctions at *Causin*, which ranks among the country's top gelaterie.

P.89 ▸ DORSODURO

▼ Paolin

There are few more pleasurable ways of whiling away an hour in Venice than sipping a drink at one of *Paolin*'s outside tables.

P.75 ▸ SAN MARCO: WEST OF THE
PIAZZA

Death in Venice

Plague-prone and swamp-bound Venice was inextricably linked with the idea of death long before Thomas Mann came along. San Michele, Santi Giovanni e Paolo and the Frari are essential sights for tomb connoisseurs, and elsewhere in the city there's plenty to interest the morbidly minded.

▼ Campo Novo

The stage-like Campo Novo, close to Santo Stefano church, is the lid of a vast pit for plague victims.

P.73 ▶ SAN MARCO: WEST OF THE PIAZZA

▼ The Lido

The beach and the grand hotels of the Lido provided the setting for Thomas Mann's great novella *Death in Venice* and Visconti's film of the book.

P.153 ▶ THE SOUTHERN ISLANDS

▶ Palazzo Vendramin-Calergi

Richard Wagner died in the Palazzo Vendramin-Calergi in February 1883; the building is now home to Venice's casino.

P.136 ▶ THE CANAL GRANDE

◀ San Simeone Profeta

The figure of Saint Simeon is a unique and unsettlingly death-touched creation.

P.98 ▶ SAN POLO AND SANTA CROCE

◀ Campo San Polo

Bullfights used to be a regular event on Campo San Polo, which also saw the murder of a member of Florence's mighty Medici clan.

P.98 ▶ SAN POLO AND SANTA CROCE

▶ San Giobbe

The church devoted to the long-suffering Job is home to one of the city's weirdest tombs.

P.109 ▶ CANNAREGIO

On the water

Water is the lifeblood of Venice, and to really appreciate the city you need to spend some time on the canals – and take a look at the site that was the foundation of the Republic's maritime power.

▲ Water-buses

The moment you arrive in Venice, buy one of the travel passes that are on offer, for unlimited use of the water-bus network.

P.175 ▶ ESSENTIALS

▲ The Arsenale

The powerhouse of the Venetian economy and the basis of its naval supremacy, the Arsenale was in effect a city within the city. Today it's mostly disused, but still redolent of former glories.

P.130 ▶ EASTERN CASTELLO

▶ Gondolas

Once an everyday means of transport round the lagoon, gondolas remain the quintessential Venetian trademark.

P.177 ▶
ESSENTIALS

▲ The Canal Grande

Get on board the #1 vaporetto for an unhurried survey of the amazing aquatic high street of Venice.

P.175 ▶ ESSENTIALS

▼ Traghetti

Can't afford a jaunt on a gondola? Never mind – hop across the Canal Grande in a stand-up traghetto instead.

P.176 ▶ ESSENTIALS

Authentic Venice

If you never stray far from the Piazza it can seem that Venice has lost much of its soul to the depredations of modern tourism. Wander just a little farther afield, however, and you'll find plentiful signs of the survival of a more traditional Venice.

▲ San Pietro di Castello

Marooned on the edge of the city, the former cathedral presides over a district where boat-maintenance is the main business.

P.131 ▸ EASTERN CASTELLO

▼ San Nicolò dei Mendicoli

Meander down to the western edge of Dorsoduro and you'll come to this quiet and ancient church, one of the most characterful in Venice.

P.85 ▸ DORSODURO

▶ Campo San Giacomo dell'Orio

The area around the church of San Giacomo dell'Orio is spacious and under-populated, as it lies off the beaten track for the majority of visitors.

P.97 ▶ SAN POLO AND SANTA CROCE

▼ Campo Santa Maria Mater Domini

With its parish church, crumbling old houses, workaday bars and artisan's workshop, Campo Santa Maria Mater Domini is like a snapshot of an earlier age.

P.94 ▶ SAN POLO AND SANTA CROCE

▶ Northern Cannaregio

On any day of the year, residents far outnumber tourists on the long canalside pavements of northern Cannaregio.

P.111 ▶ CANNAREGIO

Venetian oddities

Maze-like, car-free and dilapidatedly durable, Venice in its entirety is a very strange place, and no matter how many times you return to the city it will never lose its aura of extreme peculiarity. Some details of the townscape, however, are stranger than others. Here are a few offbeat features that are bound to stick in the memory.

▼ The Ospedaletto

From the grotesque decoration of its facade you might never guess that the Ospedaletto is actually a church.

P.121 ▶ CENTRAL CASTELLO

▼ The Scala del Bovolo

The spiralling Scala del Bovolo is featured on thousands of postcards, but few visitors to the city ever manage to find it.

P.66 ▶ SAN MARCO: NORTH OF THE PIAZZA

▲ Venetian dialect signs

The Venetian habit of dissolving consonants and dropping syllables can produce some baffling names, none more so than San Zandegolà, or San Giovanni Decollato – St John the Beheaded

P.97 ▸ SAN POLO AND SANTA CROCE

◀ Leaning Towers

In a city built on mud it's inevitable that some of the taller structures – such as the campanile of Santo Stefano – should lurch a few degrees off the perpendicular.

P.73 ▸ SAN MARCO: WEST OF THE PIAZZA

▼ Santa Maria del Giglio

The church of St Mary of the Lily is a monument to the glory of the people who paid for it rather than to the glory of God.

P.71 ▸ SAN MARCO: WEST OF THE PIAZZA

Crime and punishment

It may not have produced monsters to compare with the Borgias and the other murderous clans of Renaissance Italy, but Venice's reputation was far from spotless: the Council of Ten was once regarded with the same sort of dread as Stalin's secret police, and the city's prisons were notorious far beyond the city's boundaries. Various sites around the city have criminal associations.

▲ Paolo Sarpi

Brilliant scientist and dauntless defender of Venice's independence from papal interference, Father Sarpi fell foul of the Vatican and was targeted by its hired assassins.

P.112 ▶ CANNAREGIO

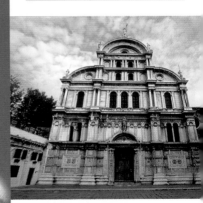

▲ Campo San Zaccaria

In the ninth century a doge was murdered outside the church of San Zaccaria; three hundred years later another doge suffered the same fate.

P.122 ▶ CENTRAL CASTELLO

▶ The Bridge of Sighs

Towards the end of your visit to the Palazzo Ducale, you cross the bridge by which prisoners were led to their cells on the other side of the canal.

P.57 ▶ SAN MARCO: THE PIAZZA

▲ La Fenice

People went to prison for burning down the opera house in 1996, but many are sceptical that the real villains have been caught.

P.71 ▶ SAN MARCO: WEST OF THE PIAZZA

▶ The Gobbo di Rialto

Misbehaving Venetians were sometimes told to report to the Gobbo di Rialto for a particularly embarrassing form of punishment.

P.93 ▶ SAN POLO AND SANTA CROCE

◀ The Piazzetta columns

Many a felon's life came to an end on the executioner's block between the twin columns of the Piazzetta, a place whose grisly aura lives on in Venetian superstition.

P.60 ▶ SAN MARCO: THE PIAZZA

Multicultural Venice

As a mercantile city, situated on the edge of the Mediterranean not far from the borders of Asia, Venice was a place where a multitude of cultures mingled. Many outsiders put down roots here; others have left fascinating evidence of their temporary residence.

▲ San Giorgio dei Greci

The precariously tilting tower marks out the church that for centuries was the spiritual centre of Venice's sizeable Greek population.

P.124 ▸ CENTRAL CASTELLO

▼ San Lazzaro degli Armeni

The Armenian island of San Lazzaro offers one of the lagoon's most intriguing guided tours, given by the monastery's multilingual residents.

P.156 ▸ SOUTHERN ISLANDS

◀ The Fondaco dei Tedeschi

Once bustling with German merchants, the Fondaco dei Tedeschi is today the city's main post office.

P.137 ▶ THE CANAL GRANDE

▶ Fondaco dei Turchi

HQ of the city's Turkish traders, the Fondaco dei Turchi is now occupied by the natural history museum.

P.97 ▶ SAN POLO & SANTA CROCE

◀ The Ghetto

The world's original ghetto is home to but a fraction of its former population, but it's still the centre of Jewish life in Venice.

P.110 ▶ CANNAREGIO

▶ Scuola degli Albanesi

Some lovely pieces of sculpture identify this tiny building as the former hub of Venice's Albanian community.

P.71 ▶ SAN MARCO: WEST OF THE PIAZZA

Festivals

Venice celebrates enthusiastically a number of special days either not observed elsewhere in Italy, or, like the Carnevale, celebrated to a lesser extent. Although they have gone through various degrees of decline and revival, the form they take now is still related very strongly to their traditional character.

▲ The Biennale

It's been going for more than a hundred years, and the Biennale remains the art world's most prestigious jamboree.

P.179 ▸ ESSENTIALS

▼ Festa della Salute

The Salute church is the centrepiece of another festival giving thanks for the restoration of the city's health (*salute*) after a terrible pestilence.

P.180 ▸ ESSENTIALS

▶ The Regata Storica

A flotilla of ornate antique boats makes its way down the Canal Grande to mark the start of the Regata Storica, the year's big event for Venice's gondoliers.

P.180 ▸ ESSENTIALS

▼ Carnevale

Italy's wildest fancy-dress party fills the ten days leading up to Shrove Tuesday and draws revellers from all over the world.

P.179 ▸ ESSENTIALS

▼ The Film Festival

Glamour and controversy always share top billing at Venice's annual film festival.

P.178 ▸ ESSENTIALS

▼ Festa del Redentore

Celebrating the city's deliverance from plague, the Redentore festival culminates with spectacular volleys of fireworks.

P.179 ▸ ESSENTIALS

Places

San Marco: the Piazza

The *sestiere* of San Marco – a rectangle smaller than 1000m by 500m – has been the nucleus of Venice from the start of the city's existence. When its founders decamped from the coastal town of Malamocco to settle on the safer islands of the inner lagoon, the area now known as the Piazza San Marco was where the first rulers built their citadel – the Palazzo Ducale – and it was here that they established their most important church – the Basilica di San Marco. Over the succeeding centuries the Basilica evolved into the most ostentatiously rich church in Christendom, and the Palazzo Ducale grew to accommodate and celebrate a system of government that endured for longer than any other republican regime in Europe. Meanwhile, the setting for these two great edifices developed into a public space so dignified that no other square in the city was thought fit to bear the name "piazza" – all other Venetian squares are campi or campielli.

Nowadays the Piazza is what keeps the city solvent: the plushest hotels are concentrated in the San Marco sestiere; the most elegant and exorbitant cafés spill out onto the pavement from the Piazza's arcades; the most extravagantly priced seafood is served in this area's restaurants; and the swankiest shops in Venice line the Piazza and the streets radiating from it.

The Basilica di San Marco

All over Venice you see images of the lion of St Mark holding a book on which is carved the text "Pax tibi, Marce evangelista meus. Hic requiescet corpus tuum" ("Peace be with you St Mark, my Evangelist. Here shall your body rest"). These supposedly are the words with which St Mark was greeted by an angel who appeared

▼ EXTERIOR OF BASILICA

San Marco: the Piazza

PLACES

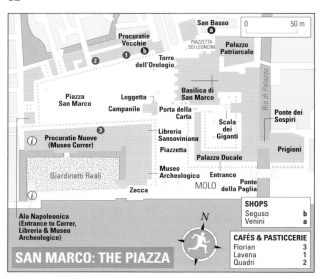

SAN MARCO: THE PIAZZA

N

SHOPS	
Seguso	b
Venini	a

CAFÉS & PASTICCERIE	
Florian	3
Lavena	1
Quadri	2

to him on the night he took shelter in the lagoon on his way back to Rome. Having thus assured themselves of the sacred ordination of their city, the first Venetians duly went about fulfilling the angelic prophecy. In 828 two merchants stole the body of Mark from its tomb in Alexandria and brought it back to Venice. Work began immediately on a shrine to house him, and the Basilica di San Marco was consecrated in 832. The amazing church you see today is essentially the version built in 1063–94, embellished in the succeeding centuries.

The marble-clad **exterior** is adorned with numerous pieces of ancient stonework, but a couple of features warrant special attention: the **Romanesque carvings** of the arches of the central doorway; and the group of porphyry figures set into the wall on the waterfront side – known as the **Tetrarchs**, in all likelihood they're a fourth-century Egyptian work depicting Diocletian and the three colleagues with whom he ruled the unravelling Roman Empire. The real **horses of San Marco** are inside the church – the four outside are modern replicas. On

Visiting San Marco

San Marco is open to tourists Monday to Saturday 9.45am–5.30pm (4.30pm from October to April) and Sunday 2–4pm, though the Loggia dei Cavalli is also open on Sunday morning. Entrance to the main part of the church is free, but admission fees totalling €6.50 are charged for certain parts of the church. You cannot take large bags into the church – they have to be left, free of charge, at nearby Calle San Basso 315a. If you're visiting San Marco in summer, get there early – by midday the queues are enormous.

▲ THE HORSES OF SAN MARCO

the main facade, the only ancient mosaic to survive is *The Arrival of the Body of St Mark*, above the **Porta di Sant'Alipio** (far left); made around 1260, it features the earliest known image of the Basilica.

Just inside, the intricately patterned stonework of the **narthex floor** is mostly eleventh- and twelfth-century, while the majority of the **mosaics** on the domes and arches constitute a series of Old Testament scenes dating from the thirteenth century. Three doges and one dogaressa have tombs in the narthex. That of Vitale Falier, the doge who consecrated the Basilica in 1094, is the oldest funerary monument in Venice – it's at the base of the first arch.

On the right of the main door from the narthex into the body of the church is a steep staircase up to the **Museo Marciano** and the **Loggia dei Cavalli** (daily: May–Sept 9.45am–5pm; Oct–April 9.45am–4pm; €3), home of the fabled horses. Thieved from Constantinople in 1204, the horses are almost certainly Roman works of the second century, and are the only *quadriga* (group of four horses

harnessed to a chariot) to have survived from the classical world.

With its undulating floor of patterned marble, its plates of eastern stone on the lower walls, and its 4000 square metres of mosaic covering every other inch of wall and vaulting, the golden **interior** of San Marco achieves a hypnotic effect. There's too much to take in at one go: the only way to do it justice is to call in for at least half an hour at the beginning and end of a couple of days. Simply to list the highlights would take pages, but be sure to make time for a good look at the following **mosaics**, nearly all of which date from the twelfth and thirteenth centuries: the west dome, showing *Pentecost*; the *Betrayal of Christ, Crucifixion, Marys at the Tomb, Descent into Limbo* and *Incredulity of Thomas*, on the arch between west and central domes; the central dome, depicting the *Ascension, Virgin with Angels and Apostles, Virtues and Beatitudes, Evangelists, Four Allegories of the Holy Rivers*; the east dome, illustrating *The Religion of Christ Foretold by the Prophets*; the *Four Patron Saints of Venice*, between the windows of

▲ THE MOSAICS

the apse (created around 1100 and thus among the earliest works in San Marco); and the huge *Agony in the Garden* on the wall of the south aisle.

Officially, the remains of St Mark lie in the sarcophagus underneath the high altar, at the back of which you can see the most precious of San Marco's treasures, the astonishing **Pala d'Oro** (May–Sept Mon–Sat 9.45am–5pm, Sun 2–4pm; Oct–April closes 4pm daily; €1.50) – the "golden altar screen". Commissioned in 976 in Constantinople, the *Pala* was enlarged, enriched and rearranged by Byzantine goldsmiths in 1105, then by Venetians in 1209 to incorporate some of the less cumbersome loot from the Fourth Crusade, and again (finally) in 1345.

Tucked into the corner of the south transept is the door of the **treasury** (same hours as Pala d'Oro; €2). This dazzling warehouse of chalices, icons, reliquaries, candelabra and other ecclesiastical appurtenances is an unsurpassed collection of Byzantine silver and gold work.

Back in the main body of the Basilica, don't overlook the **pavement** – laid out in the twelfth and thirteenth centuries, it's an intriguing patchwork of abstract shapes and religious symbols. Another marvel is the **rood screen**, surmounted by marble figures of the Virgin, St Mark and the Apostles (1394) by Jacobello and Pietro Paolo dalle Masegne. Finally, Venice's most revered religious image, the tenth-century **Icon of the Madonna of Nicopeia**, stands in the chapel on the east side of the north transept; until 1204 it was one of the most revered icons in Constantinople, where it used to be carried ceremonially at the head of the emperor's army.

The Palazzo Ducale

Daily: April–Oct 9am–7pm; Nov–March 9am–5pm. Entrance only with Museum Card. Architecturally, the Palazzo Ducale is a unique mixture: the style of its exterior, with its geometrically patterned stonework and continuous tracery walls, can only be called Islamicized Gothic, whereas the courtyards and much of the interior are based on Classical forms – a blending of influences that led Ruskin to declare it "the central building of the world". Unquestionably, it is the finest secular building of its era in Europe, and the central building of Venice: it was the residence of the doge, the home of all of Venice's governing councils, its law courts, a sizeable number of its civil servants and even its prisons. All power in the Venetian Republic and its domains was controlled within this building.

The original doge's fortress was founded at the start of the

The government of Venice

Virtually from the beginning, the **government of Venice** was dominated by the merchant class, who in 1297 enacted a measure known as the **Serrata del Maggior Consiglio** (Closure of the Great Council). From then onwards, any man not belonging to one of the wealthy families on the list compiled for the *Serrata* was ineligible to participate in the running of the city. After a while, this list was succeeded by a register of patrician births and marriages called the **Libro d'Oro**, upon which all claims to membership of the elite were based. By the second decade of the fourteenth century, the constitution of Venice had reached a form that was to endure until the coming of Napoleon; its civil and criminal code, defined in the early thirteenth century, was equally resistant to change.

What made the political system stable was its web of counterbalancing councils and committees, and its exclusion of any youngsters. Most patricians entered the Maggior Consiglio at 25 and could not expect a middle-ranking post before 45; from the middle ranks to the top was another long haul – the average age of the **doge** (see p.56) from 1400 to 1600 was 72.

ninth century, but it was in the fourteenth and fifteenth centuries that the Palazzo Ducale acquired its present shape. The principal entrance, the **Porta della Carta**, was commissioned in 1438 by Doge Francesco Fóscari, and is one of the most ornate Gothic works in the city. The passageway into the Palazzo ends under the **Arco Fóscari**, which you can see only after getting your ticket, as tourists are nowadays directed in through the arcades on the lagoon side.

From the ticket office you're directed straight into the **Museo dell'Opera**, where the originals of most of the superb capitals from the external loggias are well displayed. On the far side of the courtyard, opposite the entrance, stands the Arco Fóscari, facing the enormous staircase called the **Scala dei Giganti**. From ground level the traffic is directed up the Scala dei Censori to the upper arcade and thence up the gilded **Scala d'Oro**, the main internal staircase of the Palazzo Ducale. A subsidiary staircase on the right leads to the **Doge's Apartments** (look

out for Titian's small fresco of *St Christopher*), then the Scala d'Oro continues up to the *secondo piano nobile*, where you soon enter the **Anticollegio**. With its pictures by Tintoretto and Veronese, this is one of the richest rooms in the Palazzo Ducale, and no doubt made a suitable impact on the emissaries who waited here for admission to the **Sala del Collegio**, where the doge and his inner cabinet met. Ruskin maintained that in no other part of the palace could you "enter so deeply into the heart of Venice", though he was referring not to the mechanics of Venetian

▼ SCALA DEI GIGANTI

▲ *PARADISO*, SALA DEL MAGGIOR CONSIGLIO

power but to the luscious cycle of ceiling paintings by Veronese.

Next door – the **Sala del Senato** – was where most major policies were determined. A motley collection of late sixteenth-century artists produced the mechanically bombastic decoration of the walls and ceiling. Paolo Veronese again appears in the **Sala del Consiglio dei Dieci**, the room in which the much-feared Council of Ten discussed matters relating to state security. The unfortunates who were summoned before the Ten had to await their grilling in the next room, the **Sala della Bussola**; in the wall is a *Bocca di Leone* (Lion's Mouth), one of the boxes into which citizens could drop denunciations for the attention of the Ten and other state bodies.

Beyond the **armoury**, the Scala dei Censori takes you back to the second floor and the **Sala del Maggior Consiglio**, the assembly hall of all the Venetian patricians eligible to participate in the running of the city. This stupendous room, with its lavishly ornate ceiling, is dominated by the immense *Paradiso*, begun at the age of 77 by Tintoretto and completed by his son Domenico. Tintoretto was also commissioned to replace the room's frieze of portraits of the first 76 doges (the series continues in the Sala dello Scrutinio), but in the event Domenico and his assistants did

The doge

The **doge** was the figurehead of the Republic rather than anything akin to its president, and numerous restrictions were placed on his activities: all his letters were read by censors, for example, and he couldn't receive foreign delegations alone. On the other hand, whereas his colleagues on the various state councils were elected for terms as brief as a month, the doge was **elected for life** and sat on all the major councils, which at the very least made him extremely influential: the dogeship was the monopoly of old men, not solely because of the celebrated Venetian respect for the wisdom of the aged, but also because a man in his seventies would have fewer opportunities to abuse the powers of the dogeship. So it was that in 1618 a certain Agostino Nani, at 63 the youngest candidate for the dogeship, feigned a life-threatening decrepitude to enhance his chances of getting the job.

the work. On the Piazzetta side the sequence is interrupted by a black veil, marking the place where **Marin Falier** would have been honoured had he not conspired against the state in 1355 and (as the lettering on the veil says) been beheaded for his crime.

A couple of rooms later, the route descends to the **Magistrato alle Leggi**, in which three works by **Hieronymus Bosch** are displayed: they were left to the Palazzo Ducale in the will of Cardinal Domenico Grimani, whose collection also provided the foundations of the city's archeological museum. The Scala dei Censori leads from here to the **Ponte dei Sospiri** (Bridge of Sighs) and the **Prigioni** (Prisons). Built in 1600, the bridge takes its popular name from the sighs of the prisoners who shuffled through its corridor. In reality, though, anyone passing this way had been let off pretty lightly. Hard cases were kept either in the sweltering **Piombi** (the Leads), under the roof of the Palazzo Ducale, or in the sodden gloom of the **Pozzi** (the Wells) in the bottom two storeys.

If you want to see the Piombi, and the rooms in which the day-to-day administration of Venice took place, take the **Itinerari Segreti del Palazzo Ducale**, a fascinating ninety-minute guided tour through the warren of offices and passageways that interlocks with the building's public rooms. (Tours in English daily at 9.55am, 10.45am & 11.35am; €12.50, €7 with Venice Card, includes entry to rest of palace. Tickets can be booked a minimum of two days in advance on ☎041.520.9070;

for the next or same day go in person to Palazzo Ducale ticket desk to check availability.)

The Campanile

Daily: April–June, Sept & Oct 9am–7.45pm; July & Aug 9am–9pm; Nov–March 9.30am–4.15pm. €6.

The Campanile began life as a combined lighthouse and belltower, and was continually modified up to 1515, the year in which the golden angel was installed on the summit. Each of its five **bells** had a distinct function: the *Marangona*, the largest, tolled the beginning and end of the working day; the *Trottiera* was a signal for members of the Maggior Consiglio to hurry along; the *Nona* rang midday; the *Mezza Terza* announced a session of the Senate; and the smallest, the *Renghiera* or *Maleficio*, gave notice of an execution. But the Campanile's most dramatic contribution to the history of the city was made on July 14, 1902, the day on which, at 9.52am, it fell down. The town councillors decided that evening that the Campanile should be rebuilt "dov'era e com'era" (where it was and how it was),

▲ THE PRISONS

▲ THE CAMPANILE

restoration of the Torre dell'Orologio is drawing to a close; when it's over, it will be possible to climb up through the innards of the tower, to the terrace from which the Moors strike the hour.

The Procuratie

Away to the left of the Torre dell'Orologio stretches the **Procuratie Vecchie**, begun around 1500 to designs by Mauro Codussi, who also designed much of the clock tower. Once the home of the **Procurators of San Marco**, whose responsibilities included the upkeep of the Basilica and the administration of the other government-owned properties, the block earned substantial rents for the city coffers: the upper floors housed some of the choicest apartments in town, while the ground floor was leased to shopkeepers and craftsmen, as is still the case.

Within a century or so, the procurators were moved across the Piazza to new premises, the **Procuratie Nuove**. When Napoleon's stepson, Eugène Beauharnais, was the Viceroy of Italy, he appropriated this building as a royal palace, and then discovered that the accommodation lacked a ballroom. He duly demolished the church of San Geminiano, which had filled part of the third side of the Piazza, and connected the Procuratie Nuove and Vecchie with a new wing, the **Ala Napoleonica**, containing the essential facility.

and a decade later, on St Mark's Day 1912, the new tower was opened, in all but minor details a replica of the original. At 99m, the Campanile is the tallest structure in the city, and from the top you can make out virtually every building, but not a single canal.

The Torre dell'Orologio

The other tower in the Piazza, the Torre dell'Orologio (Clock Tower), was built between 1496 and 1506. Legend relates that the makers of the clock slaved away for three years at their project, only to have their eyes put out so that they couldn't repeat their engineering marvel for other patrons. In fact the pair received a generous pension – presumably too dull an outcome for the city's folklorists. The tower's roof terrace supports two bronze wild men known as "The Moors", because of their dark patina. A protracted

The Correr and archeological museums

Daily: April–Oct 9am–7pm; Nov–March 9am–5pm. Entrance only with Museum Card. Many of the rooms in the Ala Napoleonica and Procuratie Nuove are now occupied by the **Museo Correr**, the civic museum of Venice, which is joined to the archeological museum and Sansovino's superb library, the Libreria Sansoviniana.

Nobody could make out that the immense Correr collection is consistently fascinating, but it incorporates a picture gallery that more than makes up for the duller stretches, and its sections on Venetian society contain some eye-opening exhibits. The first floor starts off with a gallery of Homeric reliefs by Canova, whose large self-portrait faces you as you enter; succeeding rooms display his *Daedalus and Icarus* (the group that made his name at the age of 21), his faux-modest *Venus Italica* and some of the rough clay models he created as first drafts for his classically poised sculptures. After that you're into the **historical collection**, which will be intermittently enlightening if your Italian is good and you already have a pretty wide knowledge of Venetian history. Then you pass through an armoury and an exhibition of small bronze sculptures before entering the **Museo Archeologico**. It's a somewhat scrappy museum, but look out for a head of Athena from the fourth century BC, a trio of wounded Gallic warriors (Roman copies of Hellenistic originals) and a phalanx of Roman emperors.

At the furthest point of the archeological museum a door opens into the hall of Sansovino's library (see p.61). Back in the Correr, a staircase beyond the sculpture section leads to the **Quadreria**, which may be no rival for the Accademia's collection but nonetheless sets out clearly the evolution of painting in Venice from the thirteenth century to around 1500, and does contain some gems, including Jacopo de'Barbari's astonishing aerial view of Venice, some remarkable pieces by Cosmè Tura and Antonello da Messina, and a roomful of work by the Bellini family. The Correr's best-known possession, however, is the **Carpaccio** painting of two terminally bored women once known as *The Courtesans*, though in fact it depicts a couple of late fifteenth-century bourgeois ladies dressed in a style at which none of their contemporaries would have raised an eyebrow. Carpaccio was once thought to be the painter of the *Portrait of a Young Man in a Red Hat*, another much-reproduced image, but it's now given to an anonymous

▲ ENTRANCE TO THE CORRER

painter from Ferrara or Bologna. The Correr also has a room of pictures from Venice's community of Greek artists, an immensely conservative group that nurtured the painter who later became known as El Greco – there's a picture by him here which you'd walk straight past if it weren't for the label.

From the Quadreria you're directed to the **Museo del Risorgimento**, which resumes the history of the city with its fall to Napoleon; then the itinerary passes through sections on Venetian festivals, crafts, trades and everyday life. Here the frivolous items are what catch the eye, especially a pair of eighteen-inch stacked shoes (as worn by the women in the Carpaccio painting), and an eighteenth-century portable hair-care kit that's the size of a suitcase. Finally you're steered down a corridor to the ballroom – a showcase for Canova's *Orpheus and Eurydice*, created in 1777, when the sculptor was still in his teens.

The Piazzetta

For much of the Republic's existence, the Piazzetta

– the open space between the Basilica and the waterfront – was the area where the councillors of Venice would gather to scheme and curry favour. The Piazzetta was also used for public executions: the usual site was the pavement between the two granite columns on the Molo, as this stretch of the waterfront is called. The last person to be executed here was one Domenico Storti, condemned to death in 1752 for the murder of his brother.

One of the columns is topped by a modern copy of a statue of **St Theodore**, the patron saint of Venice when it was dependent on Byzantium; the original, now on show in a corner of one of the Palazzo Ducale's courtyards, was a compilation of a Roman torso, a head of Mithridates the Great and miscellaneous bits and pieces carved in Venice in the fourteenth century (the dragon included). The **winged lion** on the other column is an ancient 3000-kilo bronze beast that was converted into a lion of St Mark by jamming a bible under its paws.

▲ THE PIAZZETTA, WITH THE FACADE OF THE BIBLIOTECA

The Libreria Sansoviniana

The Piazzetta is flanked by the Libreria Sansoviniana, also known as the Biblioteca Marciana. The impetus to build the library came from the bequest of Cardinal Bessarion, who left his celebrated hoard of classical texts to the Republic in 1468. Bessarion's books and manuscripts were first housed in San Marco and then in the Palazzo Ducale, but finally it was decided that a special building was needed. Jacopo Sansovino got the job, but the library wasn't finished until 1591, two decades after his death. Contemporaries regarded the Libreria as one of the supreme designs of the era, and the **main hall** (entered from the archeological museum – see p.59) is certainly one of the most beautiful rooms in the city: paintings by Veronese, Tintoretto, Andrea Schiavone and others cover the walls and ceiling.

The Zecca

Attached to the Libreria, with its main facade to the lagoon, is Sansovino's first major building in Venice, the Zecca or Mint. Constructed in stone and iron to make it fireproof (most stonework in Venice is just skin-deep), it was built between 1537 and 1545 on the site occupied by the mint since the thirteenth century. The rooms are now part of the library, but are not open to tourists.

The Giardinetti Reali

Beyond the Zecca, and behind a barricade of postcard and toy gondola sellers, is a small public garden – the Giardinetti Reali – created by Eugène Beauharnais on the site of the state granaries. It's the nearest place to the centre where you'll find a bench and the shade of a tree, but in summer it's about as peaceful as a school playground. The spruced-up building at the foot of the nearby bridge is the Casino da Caffè, another legacy of the Napoleonic era, now the city's main tourist office.

Shops

Seguso

Piazza S. Marco 143 ⓦ www .seguso.it. Daily 10am–7pm. Traditional-style Murano glass, much of it created by the firm's founder, Archimede Seguso.

Venini

Piazzetta dei Leoncini 314 ⓦ www .venini.com. Daily 9.30am–5.30pm. One of the more adventurous glass producers, Venini often employs designers from other fields of the applied arts.

Cafés and pasticcerie

Florian

Piazza S. Marco 56–59. Closed Wed in winter. Opened in 1720 by Florian Francesconi, and frescoed and mirrored in a passable pastiche of that period, this has long been the café to be seen in. A simple cappuccino will set you back around €8; if the resident musicians are playing, you'll be taxed another €4.50.

Lavena

Piazza S. Marco 133–134. Closed Tues in winter. Wagner's favourite café (there's a commemorative plaque inside) is the second

▲ FLORIAN

member of the Piazza's top-bracket trio. For privacy you can take a table in the narrow little gallery overlooking the bar. Prices are infinitesimally lower than *Florian*'s, but the coffee is maybe even better.

Quadri

Piazza S. Marco 120–124. Closed Mon in winter. Austrian officers patronized *Quadri* during the occupation, while the natives stuck with *Florian*, and it still has something of the air of being a runner-up in the society stakes. It is nonetheless highly stylish, and the coffee is superb.

San Marco: North of the Piazza

From the Piazza the bulk of the pedestrian traffic flows north to the Rialto bridge along the Mercerie, the most aggressive and browser-choked shopping mall in Venice. Only the churches of San Giuliano and San Salvador provide a diversion from the shops until you come to the Campo San Bartolomeo, the forecourt of the Rialto bridge and one of the locals' favoured spots for an after-work chat. Another square that's lively at the end of the day is the Campo San Luca, within a minute's stroll of Al Volto, the best-stocked enoteca in town. Secreted in the folds of the alleyways hereabouts is the spiralling staircase called the Scala del Bovolo. And slotted away in a tiny square close to the Canal Grande you'll find the most delicate of Venice's museum buildings – the Palazzo Pésaro degli Orfei, home of the Museo Fortuny.

The Mercerie and San Giuliano

The Mercerie, a chain of streets that starts under the Torre dell'Orologio and finishes at the Campo San Bartolomeo, is the most direct route between San Marco and the Rialto and has always been a prime site for Venice's shopkeepers – its mixture of slickness and tackiness ensnares more shoppers than any other part of Venice. (Each of the five links in the chain is a *merceria*: Merceria dell'Orologio, di San Zulian, del Capitello, di San Salvador and 2 Aprile.) Keep your eye open for one quirky feature: over the Sottoportego del Cappello (first left after the Torre) is a relief known as

La Vecia del Morter – the Old Woman of the Mortar. The event it commemorates happened on the night of June 15, 1310, when the occupant of this house, an old woman named Giustina Rossi, looked out of her window and saw a contingent of Bajamonte Tiepolo's rebel army passing below. Possibly by accident, she

▼ FACADE OF SAN GIULIANO

SHOPS		HOTELS	
Daniela Ghezzo Segalin	e	Ai Do Mori	B
Diesel	a	Al Gambero	A
Fantoni	d	Casa Petrarca	C
Goldoni	b	Noemi	E
Paolo Olbi	f	Orseolo	D
Testolini	g		
Venetia Studium	c		

BARS & SNACKS		CAFÉS, PASTICCERIE & GELATERIA	
Alla Botte	2	Igloo	11
Al Volto	6	Marchini	9
Bácaro Jazz	1	Rosa Salva	4 & 10
Torino	8		
Vitae	7		

RESTAURANTS	
Al Conte Pescaor	5
Rosticceria Gislon	3

0   100 m

knocked a stone mortar from her sill, and the missile landed on the skull of the standard-bearer, killing him outright. Seeing their flag go down, Tiepolo's troops panicked and fled.

Farther on is the church of San Giuliano or San Zulian (Mon–Sat 8.30am–noon & 3–6pm), rebuilt in the mid-sixteenth century with the generous aid of the physician Tommaso Rangone. His munificence and intellectual brilliance are attested by the Greek and Hebrew inscriptions on the facade and by Alessandro Vittoria's portrait statue above the door.

San Salvador

Mon–Sat 9am–noon & 3–7pm.

At their far end, the Mercerie veer right at the church of San Salvador or Salvatore, which was consecrated in 1177 by Pope Alexander III. The facade is less interesting than the interior, where, on the right-hand wall, you'll find Titian's *Annunciation* (1566), signed *"Fecit, fecit"* (Painted it, painted it) supposedly to emphasize the wonder of his continued creativity in extreme old age; a scrap of paper on the rail in front of the picture records the death of the artist on August 25, 1576. Titian also painted the main altarpiece, a *Transfiguration*.

The end of the right transept is filled by the **tomb** of **Caterina Cornaro**, one of the saddest figures in Venetian history. Born into one of Venice's pre-eminent families, she became Queen of Cyprus by marriage, and after her husband's death was forced to surrender the strategically crucial island to the doge. On her return home she was led in triumph up the Canal Grande, as though her abdication had been voluntary, and then was presented with possession of the town of Ásolo as a token of the city's gratitude. She died in 1510, and this tomb erected at the end of the century.

Campo San Bartolomeo

Campo San Bartolomeo, terminus of the Mercerie, is at its best in the evening, when it is as packed as any bar in town. To show off their new wardrobe the Venetians take themselves off to the Piazza, but Campo San Bartolomeo is a spot just to meet friends and talk. A handful of bars are scattered about, but it's really the atmosphere you come for. The restoration of the **church of San Bartolomeo** (Tues, Thurs & Sat 10am–noon) has at last been completed after many years, but access is limited because it's in effect become the property of the musicians who use the building for their recitals, just as at the Pietà (see p.124). Its best paintings – organ panels by Sebastiano del Piombo – will remain in the Accademia for the foreseeable future.

Campo San Luca and Bacino Orseolo

If the crush of San Bartolomeo is too much for you, you can retire to Campo San Luca (past the front of San Salvatore and straight on), another open-air social centre, where market traders set up their stalls from time to time, temporarily shifting the campo's centre of gravity away from the fast-food outlets. From Campo San Luca, Calle Goldoni is a direct route back to the Piazza, via the Bacino Orseolo – the city's major **gondola depot**, and one of the few places where you can admire the streamlining and balance of the boats without being hassled by their owners.

Campo Manin and the Scala del Bovolo

Campo Manin – where, unusually, the most conspicuous building is a modern one, Pier Luigi Nervi's Cassa di Risparmio di Venezia – was enlarged in 1871 to make room for the monument to Daniele Manin, the lawyer who led a revolt against the Austrian occupation in 1848–49. On the wall of the alley on the south side of Campo Manin, a sign directs you to the staircase known as the Scala del Bovolo (a *bovolo* is a snail shell in Venetian dialect). External

staircases, developed originally as a way of saving space inside the building, were a common feature of Venetian houses into the sixteenth century, but this specimen, dating from around 1500, is the most flamboyant variation on the theme. You can pay to go up the staircase, escorted by a guide (April–Oct daily 10am–6pm; Nov–April Sat & Sun 10am–4pm; €3.50), but the view of it is rather more striking than the view from it.

The Museo Fortuny

The Museo Fortuny is close at hand, hidden away in a campo you'd never accidentally pass – take either of the bridges out of the Campo Manin, turn first right, and keep going. Born in Catalonia, **Mariano Fortuny** (1871–1949) is famous chiefly for the body-clinging silk dresses he created, which were so finely pleated that they could be threaded through a wedding ring, it was claimed. However, Fortuny was also a painter, architect,

▲ COURTYARD OF MUSEO FORTUNY

engraver, photographer, theatre designer and sculptor, and the contents of this rickety and atmospheric palazzo reflect his versatility, with ranks of exotic landscapes, pin-up nudes, terracotta portrait busts, stage machinery and so forth. The museum is open only for special exhibitions of design and photography, however, and it's rare for the whole of the palazzo to be visitable.

Shops

Daniela Ghezzo Segalin

Calle dei Fuseri 4365. Mon–Fri 9.30am–1pm & 3.30–7.30pm, Sat 9am–1pm. Established in 1932 by Antonio Segalin then run by his son Rolando until 2003, this workshop is now operated by Rolando's star pupil Daniela Ghezzo, who produces wonderful handmade shoes, from sturdy brogues to whimsical Carnival footwear. A pair of Ghezzos will set you back at least €500.

Diesel

Salizzada Pio X 5315 ⓦwww.diesel .com. Mon–Sat 10am–7.30pm, Sun 11am–7pm. Diesel is a rarity among the designer shops of the Mercerie area, in that it is a company from the Veneto, and this is their flagship store.

Fantoni

Salizzada S. Luca 4119. Mon–Sat 10am–8pm. For the glossiest, weightiest and most expensive art books.

Goldoni

Calle dei Fabbri 4742. Mon 2–7pm, Tues–Sat 10am–7pm. Perhaps the best general bookshop in the city; also keeps an array of maps and posters.

▲ DIESEL

Paolo Olbi

Calle della Mandola 3653; daily: April–Oct 10am–7.30pm; rest of year 10am–12.30pm & 3.30–7.30pm. Campo S. Maria Nova; daily 9am– 12.30pm & 3.30–7.30pm. The founder of this shop was largely responsible for the revival of paper marbling in Venice; today it sells a whole range of marbled stationery. There's a second branch at Campo Santa Maria Nova 6061 (Cannaregio).

Testolini

Fondamenta Orseolo 1746–47 & 1756 ⓦwww.testolini.it. Mon–Sat 9am–7pm. The city's best-known stationers, with a vast range of paper, pens, briefcases, etc. Fine art materials are sold at the branch at no.1756.

Venetia Studium

Merceria S. Zulian 723 ⓦwww .venetiastudium.com. Mon–Sat 9.30am–7.30pm, Sun 10.30am–6pm. Genuine Fortuny creations cost a fortune, but Venetia Studium sells well-priced lamps, bags and scarves in Fortuny-style pleated velour and crepe. There are two other branches in the San Marco *sestiere* – at Calle Larga

▲ MARCHINI

XXII Marzo 2403, west of the Piazza; and Calle del Lovo 4755, a short distance west of San Salvador church – and another over in San Polo, at Campo dei Frari 3006.

Cafés, pasticcerie and gelaterie

Igloo
Calle della Mandola 3651. Closed Jan & Dec; rest of year open daily. Luscious home-made ice cream to take away.

Marchini
Calle Spadaria 676. Open daily 9am–8pm. The most delicious and most expensive of Venetian *pasticciere*, where people come on Sunday morning to buy family treats. The cakes are fabulous, as is the *Marchini* chocolate.

Rosa Salva
Merceria S. Salvador 5020 & Calle Fiubera 951. Closed Sun. Excellent coffee (the city's best, many would say), and very good pastries – but for a less businesslike ambience, check out the Rosa Salva over at Zanipolo (see p.125).

Restaurants

Al Conte Pescaor
Piscina S. Zulian 544 ☎041.522.1483. Closed Sun. A fine (if pricey) and well-reputed little fish restaurant – if you're looking for a good meal within a stone's throw of the Piazza, this is the place.

Rosticceria Gislon
Calle della Bissa 5424a. Daily 9am– 9.30pm. Downstairs it's a sort of glorified snack bar, serving pizzas and set meals starting at around €10 – the trick is to first grab a place at one of the long tables along the windows, then order from the counter. Good if you need to refuel quickly and cheaply, but can't face another pizza. There's a less rudimentary restaurant upstairs, where prices are considerably higher for no great increase in quality.

Bars and snacks

Alla Botte
Calle della Bissa 5482. Closed Wed eve and Sun. Well-hidden tiny *bacaro*, just off Campo San Bartolomeo, offering an excellent spread of *cicheti*. Calle della Bissa is one of the most confusing alleyways in

Venice – to find *Alla Botte*, take either of the alleys labelled Calle della Bissa (on the east side of the campo), turn first left and go as straight as you can.

Al Volto

Calle Cavalli 4081. Closed Sun.

This dark little bar is an *enoteca* in the true sense of the word, with 1300 wines from Italy and elsewhere, a hundred of them served by the glass, some cheap, many not; good snacks, too.

Bácaro Jazz

Salizzada Fondaco dei Tedeschi 5546. Open 4pm–3am, closed Wed.

A jazz-themed bar that's proved a big hit with cool Venetian kids, not least because of its very late hours. The food can be dodgy, though.

Torino

Campo S. Luca 4591. Open until 1am, closed Sun & Mon.

Lively and loud bar, with live jazz sessions on Wednesdays. Good for sandwiches, or more substantial food at lunchtime.

Vitae

Calle Sant'Antonio 4118. Open 9am–2am, closed Sun.

Trendy and tiny new bar to the north of Campo Manin, serving superb cocktails.

San Marco: West of the Piazza

Leaving the Piazza by the west side you enter another major shopping district, but one that presents a contrast to the frenetic Mercerie: here the clientele is drawn predominantly from the city's well-heeled or from the five-star tourists staying in the hotels that overlook the end of the Canal Grande – though in recent years it's also become a favourite pitch for African street traders. To a high proportion of visitors, this part of the city is principally the place to go buying Gucci or Armani, or is merely the route to the Accademia, but there are things to see here apart from the latest creations from Milan and Paris – the extraordinary Baroque facades of Santa Maria del Giglio and San Moisè, for instance, or the graceful Santo Stefano, which rises at the end of one of the largest and most attractive squares in Venice.

San Moisè

Daily 3.30–7pm, plus Sun 9am–noon.

San Moisè, which was founded in the eighth century, would be

▼ FACADE OF SAN MOISÈ

the runaway winner of any poll for the ugliest church in Venice. The church's name means "Saint Moses", the Venetians here following the Byzantine custom of canonizing Old Testament figures, while simultaneously honouring Moisè Venier, who paid for a rebuilding way back in the tenth century. Its delirious facade sculpture was created in 1668 by Heinrich Meyring; and if you think this bloated display of fauna and flora is in questionable taste, wait till you see the miniature mountain he carved as the main altarpiece, representing *Mount Sinai with Moses Receiving the Tablets*.

Calle Larga XXII Marzo

If you're looking for an escritoire for your drawing room, an oriental carpet for the reception area, a humble Dutch landscape or a new designer suit, then you'll probably find what you're after on or around the broad Calle Larga XXII Marzo, which begins over the canal from San Moisè. Many of the streets off the western side of the Piazza are dedicated to the beautification of the prosperous and their dwellings, with names such as Versace, Gucci, Ferragamo, Prada and Vuitton lurking round every corner.

La Fenice

Halfway along Calle Larga XXII Marzo, on the right, Calle del Sartor da Veste takes you over a canal and into **Campo San Fantin**. The square is dominated by the Teatro la Fenice, Venice's oldest and largest theatre. Giannantonio Selva's gaunt Neoclassical design was not deemed a great success on its inauguration on December 26, 1792, but nonetheless very little of the exterior was changed when the place had to be rebuilt after a fire in 1836. Similarly, when La Fenice was again destroyed by fire on the night of January 29, 1996, it was decided to rebuild it as a replica of Selva's theatre: after all, its acoustics were superb and – with a capacity of just nine hundred people – it had an inspiringly intimate atmosphere. La Fenice saw some significant musical events in the twentieth century – Stravinsky's *The Rake's Progress* and Britten's *The Turn of the Screw* were both premiered here – but the music scene was more exciting in the nineteenth century, when, in addition to staging the premieres of operas by Rossini, Bellini and Verdi (*Rigoletto* and *La Traviata* both opened here), it became the focal point for protests against the occupying Austrian army. For information on tickets for performances, see p.77.

Santa Maria del Giglio

Mon–Sat 10am–5pm, Sun 1–5pm.
€2.50, or Chorus Pass.

Back on the route to the Accademia, another extremely odd church awaits – Santa Maria del Giglio (Mary of the Lily), more commonly known as Santa Maria Zobenigo, an alternative title derived from the name of the family who founded it in the ninth century. The exterior features not a single unequivocally Christian image: the main statues are of the five **Barbaro** brothers, who financed the rebuilding of the church in 1678; Virtue, Honour, Fame and Wisdom hover at a respectful distance; and relief maps at eye level depict the towns distinguished with the brothers' presence in the course of their military and diplomatic careers. The interior, full to bursting with devotional pictures and sculptures, overcompensates for the impiety of the exterior.

San Maurizio and the Scuola degli Albanesi

The tilting campanile of Santo Stefano (see below) looms into view over the vapid and deconsecrated church of San Maurizio, which is used as an exhibition space (currently it houses a display of Baroque musical instruments; daily 9.30am–8.30pm; free). A few metres away, at the head of Calle del Piovan, stands a diminutive building that was once the Scuola degli Albanesi, the confraternity of the city's Albanian community; it was established in 1497 and the reliefs on the facade date from shortly after that.

Campo Santo Stefano

The church of Santo

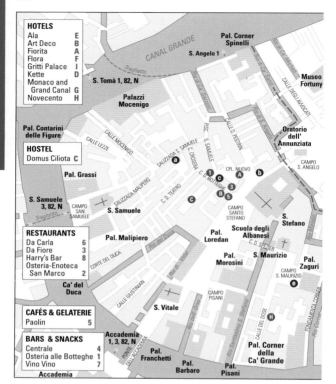

HOTELS

Ala	E
Art Deco	B
Fiorita	A
Flora	F
Gritti Palace	I
Kette	D
Monaco and Grand Canal	G
Novecento	H

HOSTEL

Domus Ciliota	C

RESTAURANTS

Da Carla	6
Da Fiore	3
Harry's Bar	8
Osteria-Enoteca San Marco	2

CAFÉS & GELATERIE

Paolin	5

BARS & SNACKS

Centrale	4
Osteria alle Botteghe	1
Vino Vino	7

Stefano closes one end of the spacious Campo Santo

Stefano. The campo has an alias – Campo Francesco

▼ CAMPO SANTO STEFANO

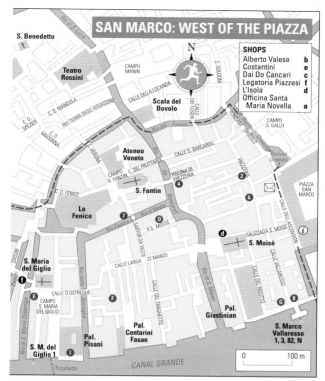

SHOPS

Alberto Valese	b
Costantini	e
Dai Do Cancari	c
Legatoria Piazzesi	f
L'Isola	d
Officina Santa Maria Novella	a

Morosini – that comes from a former inhabitant of the **palazzo** at no. 2802. The last doge to serve as military commander of the Republic (1688–94), **Francesco Morosini** became a Venetian hero with his victories in the Peloponnese, but is notorious elsewhere as the man who lobbed a missile through the roof of the Parthenon in Athens, detonating the Turkish gunpowder that had been stored there.

The church of **Santo Stefano** (Mon–Sat 10am–5pm, Sun 1–5pm) is notable for its Gothic doorway and beautiful **ship's keel roof**, both of which date from the fifteenth century, the last phase of the church's construction. The airy and calm interior is one of the most pleasant places in Venice just to sit and think, but it also contains some major works of art, notably in the picture-packed sacristy (€2.50, or Chorus Pass), where you'll find a *St Lawrence* and a *St Nicholas of Bari* by Bartolomeo Vivarini, a Crucifix by Paolo Veneziano, and a trio of late works by Tintoretto.

Campo Novo

Nearby Campo Novo was formerly the churchyard of Santo Stefano, and was used as a burial pit during the catastrophic plague of 1630. Such was the volume of corpses interred here that for health reasons the site remained closed to the public from then until 1838.

Palazzo Pisani

Campiello Pisani, at the back of Morosini's house, is a forecourt to the Palazzo Pisani, one of the biggest houses in the city, and now the Conservatory of Music. Work began on it in the early seventeenth century and continued for over a century; it was at last brought to a halt by the government, who decided that the Pisani, among the city's richest banking families, were getting ideas above their station.

San Samuele and Palazzo Grassi

From opposite the entrance to Santo Stefano church, Calle delle Botteghe and Crosera lead up to Salizzada San Samuele, a route that takes you past the house in which Paolo Veronese lived his final years, and on to Campo San Samuele. Built in the late twelfth century and not much altered since, the **campanile** of San Samuele is one of the oldest in the city. The church itself – largely reconstructed in the late seventeenth century – is dwarfed by the Palazzo Grassi, which became famous in the twenty years it was run by Fiat for blockbusting exhibitions on subjects such as the Celts, the Pharaohs and the Phoenicians. In 2005 it was acquired by the phenomenally wealthy François Pinault, who hired the Japanese architect Tadao Ando to reconfigure the interior. In addition, Pinault has undertaken to restore the small eighteenth-century theatre beside the Grassi, to house a frequently changing sample of his vast collection of modern art, which ranges from Picasso, Miró and Mondrian to contemporaries such as Jeff Koons, Maurizio Cattelan and Mario Merz. Works owned by Pinault will be central to future Grassi exhibitions, but the shows will still feature pan-cultural exhibitions of the sort that made the Grassi renowned.

▼ ALBERTO VALESE

Shops

Alberto Valese

Campo S. Stefano 3471, ⑩ www.albertovalese-ebru .com. Mon–Sat 10am– 1.30pm & 2.30–7pm, Sun 11am–6pm. Valese not only produces the most luscious marbled papers in Venice, but also transfers the designs onto silk scarves and a variety of ornaments; the marbling technique he uses is a Turkish process called *ebrû* (meaning cloudy) – hence the alternative name of his shop.

Costantini

Campo S. Maurizio 2668a. Mon–Fri 3.30–7.30pm, Sat 11am–6.30pm. Large array of *perle veneziane* (glass beads) sold individually, made into jewellery or by the bag according to weight.

Dai Do Cancari

Calle delle Botteghe 3455. Tues–Sat 10am–7pm. Perhaps Venice's best wine shop, selling scores of the country's finest vintages, as well as cheap draught wine (*vino sfuso*).

Legatoria Piazzesi

Campiello della Feltrina 2511. Mon–Sat 10am–7pm. Located near Santa Maria Zobenigo, this paper-producer was founded way back in 1828 and claims to be the oldest such shop in Italy. Using the old wood-block method of printing, it makes stunning hand-printed papers and cards, and a nice line in pocket diaries, too.

L'Isola

Salizzada S. Moisè 1468 ⓦ www .carlomoretti.com. Daily 9am–7pm. Chiefly a showcase for work by Carlo Moretti, the doyen of modernist Venetian glass artists.

Officina Profumo-Farmaceutica Santa Maria Novella

Salizzada S. Samuele 3149 ⓦ www .smnovella.it. Mon–Sat 10am–1pm & 2–7pm. The Venetian branch of the famous Florentine operation, founded in the sixteenth century by Dominican monks as an outlet for their potions and herbal remedies. Many of these are still available, including distillations of flowers and herbs, together with face-creams, shampoos, soaps and wondrous aromatics for the body and home.

Cafés and gelaterie

Paolin

Campo S. Stefano 2962. Closed Fri. The outside tables of *Paolin* enjoy one of the finest settings in the city, and their ice cream is regarded by many as the best in Venice.

Restaurants

Da Carla

Sottoportego Corte Contarina 1535a ☎ 041.523.7855. Closed Sun. The battered old sign is somewhat misleading, as this tiny bar-*trattoria*, hidden down a sottoportego off the west side of Frezzeria, has recently undergone a makeover, but it's still packed at lunchtimes with workers dropping in for sandwiches, simple pasta dishes and salads. One of the best places for a quick bite close to the Piazza.

Da Fiore

Calle delle Botteghe 3461 ☎ 041.523.5310. Closed Tues. This popular mid-range restaurant offers genuine Venetian cuisine in a classy *trattoria*-style setting. The anteroom is a nice small bar that does very good *cicheti*.

Harry's Bar

Calle Vallaresso 1323 ☎ 041.528.5777. Open daily.

▲ OSTERIA ALLE BOTTEGHE

Often described as the most reliable of the city's gourmet restaurants (*carpaccio* – raw strips of thin beef – was first created here), though there are sceptics who think the place's reputation has more to do with glamour than cuisine. The bar itself is famed in equal measure for its cocktails, its sandwiches and its phenomenal prices. It's *the* place to sample a *Bellini* (fresh white peach juice and *prosecco*), which was invented here.

Osteria-Enoteca San Marco

Frezzeria 1610 ☎041.528.5242. Closed Sun. As you'd expect for a place so close to the Piazza, this classy modern *osteria* is cetainly not cheap, but prices are not madly unreasonable for the quality of the food – and the attitude of the place makes a change from the cynicism you too often encounter in San Marco restaurants. The wine list is very good too.

Bars and snacks

Centrale Restaurant Lounge

Piscina Frezzeria 1659b ☎041.296. 0664. Open 6.30pm–2am; closed Tues. The spacious, transatlantic-style *Centrale* touts itself as the best-designed and coolest bar-restaurant in town, and few would argue with the claim. The food is very expensive (you'll pay around €70 per person), but you might be tempted to blow a few euros for the pleasure of sinking into one of the sumptuous leather soafs, cocktail in hand, and listening to late-night jazz or "music chillout".

Osteria alle Botteghe

Calle delle Botteghe 3454. Closed Sun. Sumptuous sandwiches and snacks; most lunchtimes you need a shoehorn to get in the place.

Vino Vino

Ponte delle Veste 2007. Open 10am–midnight; closed Tues.

Very close to the Fenice opera house, this wine bar stocks more than 350 wines. It serves relatively inexpensive meals as well.

Opera & classical music

La Fenice

Campo S. Fantin, ⓦwww .teatrolafenice.it. La Fenice, the third-ranking Italian opera house after Milan's La Scala and Naples' San Carlo, is also a venue for smaller-scale events, which are held in the theatre's Sale Apollinee. Prices in the main house start at a mere €10, but these seats give no view of the stage; good seats can be had for a reasonable €50–60, except on premiere nights, when prices are almost doubled. The opera season runs from late November to the end of June, punctuated by ballet performances. Tickets can be bought at the Fenice box office, the Piazza tourist office, the VeLa/ACTV offices at Piazzale Roma and the train station and at Vivaldi Store, opposite the post office in Salizzada Fontego dei Tedeschi.

Dorsoduro

There were not many places among the lagoon's mud-banks where Venice's early settlers could be confident that their dwellings wouldn't slither down into the water, but with Dorsoduro they were on relatively solid ground: the sestiere's name translates as "hard back", and its buildings occupy the largest area of firm silt in the centre of the city. The main draw here is the Gallerie dell'Accademia, the city's top art gallery, while the most conspicuous building is the huge church of Santa Maria della Salute, the grandest gesture of Venetian Baroque. In terms of artistic contents, the Salute takes second place to San Sebastiano, the parish church of Paolo Veronese. Giambattista Tiepolo, the master colourist of a later era, is well represented at the Scuola Grande dei Carmini, and for an overall view of Tiepolo's cultural milieu there's the Ca' Rezzonico, home of Venice's museum of eighteenth-century art and artefacts. Art of the twentieth century is also in evidence – at the Guggenheim Collection, which is small yet markedly superior to the city's public collection of modern art in the Ca' Pésaro (see p.94).

The Accademia

Ⓦ www.gallerieaccademia.org; Mon 8.15am–2pm, Tues–Sun 8.15am–7.15pm. €6.50. The Gallerie dell'Accademia is one of the obligatory tourist sights in Venice, but until the construction of its new galleries has been completed admissions will continue to be restricted to three hundred people at a time. Accordingly, if you're visiting in summer and don't want to wait for hours, get there well before the doors open or at about 1pm, when most people are having lunch.

The first room of the Accademia's generally chronological arrangement is filled with pieces by the earliest-known individual Venetian painters, Paolo Veneziano and his follower Lorenzo Veneziano.

Beyond here, room 2 is given over to large altarpieces from the late fifteenth and early sixteenth centuries, including works by Giovanni Bellini, Cima da Conegliano and Vittore Carpaccio. Carpaccio's strange *Crucifixion and Glorification of the Ten Thousand Martyrs of Mount Ararat* is the most gruesome painting in the room, and the most charming is by him too: *The Presentation of Jesus in the Temple*, with its pretty, wingless, lute-playing angel.

The beginnings of the Venetian obsession with the way in which forms are defined by light and the emergence of the characteristically soft and rich Venetian palette are seen in rooms 3, 4 and 5, the last two of which are a high point of the Accademia. Outstanding are an exquisite *St George* by **Mantegna** (c.1466), a series of *Madonnas* and a *Pietà* by **Giovanni Bellini**, and two pieces by the most mysterious of Italian painters, **Giorgione** – his *Portrait of an Old Woman* and the so-called *Tempest* (c.1500).

Rooms 6 to 8 mark the entry of Tintoretto, Titian and Veronese, the heavyweights of the Venetian High Renaissance. These works would be the prize of many other collections, but here they are just appetizers for what's to come in the huge room 10, one whole wall of which is needed for *Christ in the House of Levi* by **Paolo Veronese**. Originally called *The Last Supper*, this picture brought down on Veronese the wrath of the Inquisition, who objected to the inclusion of "buffoons, drunkards, Germans, dwarfs, and similar indecencies" in the sacred scene. Veronese's insouciant response was simply to change the title, an emendation that apparently satisfied his critics. Among the works by **Tintoretto** is the painting that made his reputation: *St Mark Freeing a Slave* (1548), showing St Mark's intervention at the execution of a slave who had defied his master by travelling to the Evangelist's shrine. Opposite is **Titian**'s highly charged *Pietà* (1576), painted for his own tomb in the Frari and completed after his death by Palma il Giovane.

In room 11 a major shift into the eighteenth century occurs, with pieces by **Giambattista Tiepolo**; his contemporaries provide the chief interest of next section, with works such as **Giambattista Piazzetta**'s extraordinary *The Fortune-Teller*, **Guardi**'s impressionistic views of Venice, **Pietro Longhi**'s documentary interiors and a series of portraits by **Rosalba Carriera**, one of the very few women shown in the collection.

After a large hall that houses numerous paintings by two of Venice's most significant artistic dynasties, the **Vivarini** and **Bellini** families, you come to **room 20**, which is entirely filled by the cycle of *The Miracles of the Relic of the Cross*. Produced by various artists (most notably Gentile Bellini) between 1494 and 1501, it was commissioned by the Scuola Grande di San Giovanni Evangelista to extol the holy fragment it had held since 1369 (see p.102).

▲ THE ACCADEMIA

PLACES Dorsoduro

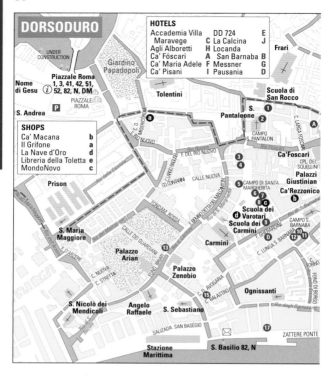

DORSODURO

HOTELS

Accademia Villa		DD 724	E
Maravege	C	La Calcina	J
Agli Alboretti	H	Locanda	
Ca' Fóscari	A	San Barnaba	B
Ca' Maria Adele	F	Messner	G
Ca' Pisani	I	Pausania	D

UNDER CONSTRUCTION

Giardino Papadopoli

Frari

Piazzale Roma
1, 3, 41, 42, 51,
Nome
di Gesu ℹ️ **52, 82, N, DM**

PIAZZALE ROMA

S. Andrea

🅿️

Scuola di San Rocco

Tolentini

S. ❶ Pantaleone ❷

C. LARGA FOSCARI

SHOPS

Ca' Macana	b
Il Grifone	a
La Nave d'Oro	d
Libreria della Toletta	e
MondoNovo	c

❽

CAMPO S. PANTALON

Rio Foscari

Ⓐ

CPL. DEI SQUELLINI

Ca'Foscari

❸

❹

Ca'Rezzonico ⓑ

Palazzi Giustinian

Prison

CAMPO DI SANTA MARGHERITA

❺

❼ ❻ Ⓒ

Scuola dei
❹ Varotari

❽

CAMPO S. BARNABA

❿

S. Maria Maggiore

Scuola dei Carmini ❾

Carmini

❿ ❶❷ ❶❶

Palazzo Arian

❶❸

Palazzo Zenobio

Ognissanti

S. Nicolò dei Mendicoli

Angelo Raffaele

S. Sebastiano

❶❼

ZATTERE PONTE

SALIZADA SAN BASÉGIO

✉️

Stazione Marittima

S. Basilio 82, N

Another remarkable cycle fills room 21 – **Carpaccio**'s *Story of St Ursula*, painted for the Scuola di Sant'Orsola at San Zanipolo in 1490–94. A

▼ THE GUGGENHEIM

superlative exercise in pictorial narrative, the paintings are especially fascinating to the modern viewer as a meticulous record of domestic architecture, costume and the decorative arts in Venice at the close of the fifteenth century. After this room, you leave the Accademia through a door beneath **Titian**'s wonderful *Presentation of the Virgin* (1539), still occupying the space for which it was painted.

The Guggenheim

ⓦ www.guggenheim-venice.it; 10am–6pm; closed Tues. €10.

The Peggy Guggenheim Collection is installed in the peculiarly modernistic fragment of the quarter-built Palazzo

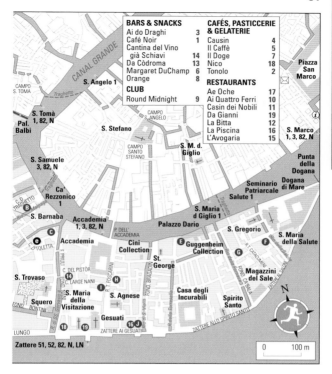

BARS & SNACKS

Ai do Draghi	3
Café Noir	1
Cantina del Vino	
già Schiavi	14
Da Còdroma	13
Margaret DuChamp	6
Orange	8

CLUB

Round Midnight	9

CAFÉS, PASTICCERIE & GELATERIE

Causin	4
Il Caffè	5
Il Doge	7
Nico	18
Tonolo	2

RESTAURANTS

Ae Oche	17
Ai Quattro Ferri	10
Casin dei Nobili	11
Da Gianni	19
La Bitta	12
La Piscina	16
L'Avogaria	15

Venier dei Leoni, a bit farther down the Canal Grande.

In the early years of the twentieth century the leading lights of the Futurist movement came here for the parties thrown by the dotty Marchesa Casati, who was fond of stunts like setting wild cats and apes loose in the palazzo garden, among plants sprayed lilac for the occasion. Peggy Guggenheim, a considerably more discerning patron of the arts, moved into the palace in 1949; since her death in 1979 the Guggenheim Foundation has administered the place, and has turned her private collection into one of the city's glossiest museums – and the second most popular after the

Accademia. It is a small but generally top-quality assembly of twentieth-century art and a prime venue for touring exhibitions. In the permanent collection the core pieces include Brancusi's *Bird in Space* and *Maestra*, De Chirico's *Red Tower* and *Nostalgia of the Poet*, Max Ernst's *Robing of the Bride* (Guggenheim was married to Ernst in the 1940s), sculpture by Laurens and Lipchitz and works by Malevich and Schwitters; other artists include Picasso, Braque, Chagall, Pollock, Duchamp, Giacometti, Picabia and Magritte. Marino Marini's *Angel of the Citadel*, out on the terrace, flaunts his erection at the passing canal traffic; more decorous pieces by

▲ SANTA MARIA DELLA SALUTE

Giacometti, Moore, Paolozzi and others are planted in the garden, surrounding Peggy Guggenheim's burial place.

Santa Maria della Salute

Daily 9am–noon & 3–6.30pm; closes 5.30pm in winter. In 1630–31 Venice was devastated by a plague that exterminated nearly 95,000 of the lagoon's population – one person in three. In October 1630 the Senate decreed that a new church would be dedicated to Mary if the city were saved, and the result was Santa Maria della Salute (*salute* meaning "health" and "salvation"). Resting on a platform of more than 100,000 wooden piles, the Salute took half a century to build; its architect, **Baldassare Longhena**, was only 26 years old when his proposal was accepted and lived just long enough to see it finished, in 1681.

Each year on November 21 (the feast of the Presentation of the Virgin) the Signoria processed from San Marco to the Salute for a service of thanksgiving, crossing the Canal Grande on a pontoon bridge laid from Santa Maria del Giglio. The Festa della Madonna della Salute is still a major event in the Venetian calendar.

The form of the Salute owes much to the plan of Palladio's Redentore (see p.152) – the obvious model for a dramatically sited votive church – and to the repertoire of Marian symbolism. The octagonal plan and eight facades allude to the eight-pointed Marian star, for example, while the huge dome represents Mary's crown and the centralized plan is a conventional symbol of the Virgin's womb. Less arcane symbolism is at work on the **high altar**, where the Virgin and Child rescue Venice (kneeling woman) from the plague (old woman); in attendance are SS Mark and Lorenzo Giustiniani, first patriarch of Venice.

The most notable paintings in the Salute are the **Titian** pieces brought from the suppressed church of Santo Spirito in Isola in 1656, and now displayed in the sacristy (€1.50). Tintoretto has included himself in the dramatis personae of his *Marriage at Cana* (1561) – he's the first Apostle on the left.

The Zàttere and the Gesuati

Known collectively as the Zàttere, the sequence of waterfront pavements between the Punta della Dogana and the Stazione Maríttima, are now a popular place for a stroll or an al fresco pizza, but were formerly the place where most of the bulky goods coming into Venice were unloaded onto floating rafts called *zàttere*.

The first building to break your stride for is the church of the Gesuati or Santa Maria del Rosario (Mon–Sat 10am–5pm, Sun 1–5pm; €2.50, or Chorus Pass). Rebuilt in 1726–43, about half a century after the church was taken over from the order of the Gesuati by the Dominicans, this was the first church designed by **Giorgio Massari**, an architect who often worked with **Giambattista Tiepolo**. Tiepolo painted the first altarpiece on the right, *The Virgin with SS Catherine of Siena, Rose and Agnes* (c.1740), and the three magnificent ceiling panels of *Scenes from the Life of St Dominic* (1737–39), which are seen to best effect in the afternoon. The third altar on this side of the church is adorned with a painting of *SS Vincent Ferrer, Giacinto and Luigi Beltran* by Tiepolo's principal forerunner, Giambattista Piazzetta; opposite, the first altar has Sebastiano Ricci's *Pius V with SS Thomas Aquinas and Peter Martyr* (1739), completing the church's array of Rococo propaganda on behalf of the exalted figures of Dominican orthodoxy, followed by a tragically intense *Crucifixion* by Tintoretto (c.1555) on the third altar.

The squero di San Trovaso

Ten thousand gondolas operated on the canals of sixteenth-century Venice, when they were the standard form of transport around the city; nowadays the tourist trade is pretty well all that sustains the city's fleet of around five hundred gondolas, which provide steady employment for a few **squeri**, as the gondola yards are called. A display in the Museo Storico Navale (see p.130) takes you through the construction of a gondola, but no abstract demonstration can equal the fascination of a working yard, and the most public one in Venice is the **squero di San Trovaso**, on the Zàttere side of San Trovaso church. The San Trovaso is the oldest *squero* still functioning – established in the seventeenth century, it looks rather like an alpine farmhouse, a reflection of the architecture of the Dolomite villages from which many of Venice's gondola-builders once came.

San Trovaso

Mon–Sat 3–6pm. Don't bother consulting your dictionary of saints for the dedicatee of San Trovaso church – the name's a baffling

▼ THE ZÀTTERE

dialect version of Santi Gervasio e Protasio. Since its tenth-century foundation the church has had a chequered history, falling down once, and twice being destroyed by fire; this is the fourth incarnation, built in 1584–1657.

Venetian folklore has it that this church was the only neutral ground between the Nicolotti and the Castellani, the two factions in to which the working-class citizens of the city were divided – the former, coming from the west and north of the city, were named after the church of San Nicolò dei Mendicoli (see opposite), the latter, from the *sestieri* of Dorsoduro, San Marco and Castello, took their name from San Pietro di Castello. The rivals celebrated inter-marriages and other services here, but are said to have entered and departed by separate doors.

Inside, San Trovaso is spacious and somewhat characterless,

but it does boast a pair of fine paintings by **Tintoretto**: *The Temptation of St Anthony* and *The Last Supper*. The former is in the chapel to the left of the high altar, with *St Crysogonus on Horseback* by **Michele Giambono** (c.1450), Venice's main practitioner of the International Gothic style; the latter is in the chapel at ninety degrees to the first one.

San Sebastiano

Mon–Sat 10am–5pm, Sun 1–5pm. €2.50, or Chorus Pass. At the end of the Záttere the barred gates of the Stazione Maríttima deflect you away from the waterfront and towards the church of San Sebastiano. The parish church of **Paolo Veronese**, it contains a group of resplendent paintings by him that gives it a place in his career comparable to that of San Rocco in the career of Tintoretto. Veronese was still in his twenties when he was asked to paint the ceiling of the **sacristy** with a *Coronation of the Virgin* and the *Four Evangelists* (1555); once that commission had been carried out, he decorated the **nave ceiling** with *Scenes from the Life of St Esther*. His next project, the dome of the chancel, was later destroyed, but the sequence he and his brother Benedetto then painted on the walls of the church and the nuns' choir at the end of the 1550s has survived in pretty good shape. In the following

▲ SAN TROVASO

decade he executed the last of the pictures, those on the **organ shutters** and around the **high altar** – on the left, *St Sebastian Leads SS Mark and Marcellian to Martyrdom* and on the right, *The Second Martyrdom of St Sebastian* (the customarily depicted torture by arrows didn't kill him). Other riches include a late **Titian** of *St Nicholas* (on the left wall of the first chapel on the right), and the early sixteenth-century majolica pavement in the chapel to the left of the chancel – in front of which is Veronese's tomb slab.

▲ SAN NICOLÒ DEI MENDICOLI

Angelo Raffaele

Mon–Fri 8am–noon & 3–5pm, Sat closes 6.30pm, Sun 9am–noon. On the far side of Campo San Sebastiano, the seventeenth-century church of Angelo Raffaele is instantly recognizable by the two huge war memorials blazoned on the canal facade. Inside, the organ loft above the entrance on the canal side is decorated with *Scenes from the Life of St Tobias* (accompanied, as ever, by his little dog), painted by one or other of the **Guardi** brothers (nobody's sure which). Although small in scale, the free brushwork and imaginative composition make the panels among the most charming examples of Venetian Rococo, a fascinating counterpoint to the grander visions of Giambattista Tiepolo, the Guardis' brother-in-law.

San Nicolò dei Mendicoli

Daily 10am–noon & 4–6pm. Although it's located on the edge of the city, the church of San Nicolò dei Mendicoli is one of Venice's oldest, said to have been founded in the seventh century. Its long history was reflected in the fact that it gave its name to the **Nicolotti** faction, whose titular head, the so-called *Gastaldo* or the *Doge dei Nicolotti*, was elected by the parishioners and then honoured by a ceremonial greeting from the Republic's doge.

The church has been rebuilt and altered at various times, and was last restored in the 1970s, when Nic Roeg used it as a setting for *Don't Look Now*. In essence, however, its shape is still that of the Veneto-Byzantine structure raised here in the twelfth century, the date of its rugged campanile. The other conspicuous feature of the exterior is the fifteenth-century porch, a type of construction once common in Venice, and often used here as makeshift accommodation for penurious nuns. The **interior**

▲ SANTA MARIA DEL CARMELO

is a miscellany of periods and styles. Parts of the apse and the columns of the nave go back to the twelfth century, but the darkened gilded woodwork that gives the interior its rather overcast appearance was installed late in the sixteenth century, as were most of the paintings, many of which were painted by Alvise dal Friso and other pupils of Paolo Veronese.

Campo di Santa Margherita

The vast, elongated Campo di Santa Margherita, ringed by houses that date back as far as the fourteenth century, is the social heart of Dorsoduro, many of whose inhabitants come here regularly to shop at its fish stalls. Students from the nearby university hang out in the campo's many bars and cafés, and the place as a whole has a vaguely alternative feel.

Just off Campo Santa Margherita's southwest tip is the **Scuola Grande dei Carmini** (daily: April–Oct 10am–5pm; Nov–March 10am–4pm; €5), once the Venetian base of the

Carmelites. Originating in Palestine towards the close of the twelfth century, the Carmelites blossomed during the Counter-Reformation, when they became the shock-troops through whom the cult of the Virgin could be disseminated, as a response to the inroads of Protestantism. As happened elsewhere in Europe, the Venetian Carmelites became immensely wealthy, and in the 1660s they called in an architect – probably Longhena – to redesign the property they had acquired. The core of this complex, which in 1767 was raised to the status of a *scuola grande* (see p.100), is now effectively a showcase for the art of **Giambattista Tiepolo**, who in the 1740s painted the wonderful ceiling of the upstairs hall.

The adjacent **Carmini** church, or Santa Maria del Carmelo (Mon–Sat 2.30–5.30pm), is a collage of architectural styles, with a sixteenth-century facade, a Gothic side doorway which preserves several Byzantine fragments, and a fourteenth-century basilican interior. A dull series of Baroque paintings illustrating the history of the Carmelite order covers a lot of space inside, but the second altar on the right has a *Nativity* by Cima da Conegliano (before 1510), and Lorenzo Lotto's *SS Nicholas of Bari, John the Baptist and Lucy* (1529) – featuring what Bernard Berenson ranked as one of the most beautiful landscapes in all Italian art – hangs on the opposite side of the nave.

San Pantaleone

Mon–Sat 8–10am & 4–6pm.

The church of San Pantaleone,

a short distance to the north of Campo Santa Margherita, has the most melodramatic **ceiling** in Venice. Painted on sixty panels, some of which actually jut out over the nave, *The Martyrdom and Apotheosis of St Pantaleone* kept **Gian Antonio Fumiani** busy from 1680 to 1704. Sadly, he never got the chance to bask in the glory of his labours – he died in a fall from the scaffolding from which he'd been working. In addition, the church possesses a fine picture by Antonio Vivarini and Giovanni d'Alemagna (in the chapel to the left of the chancel) and Veronese's last painting, *St Pantaleone Healing a Boy* (second chapel on right).

The Ponte dei Pugni and San Barnaba

Cutting down the side of the Carmini church takes you over the Rio di San Barnaba, along which a fondamenta runs to the church of San Barnaba. Just before the end of the fondamenta you pass the Ponte dei Pugni, one of several bridges with this name. Originally built without parapets, they were the sites of ritual battles between the Castellani and Nicolotti; this one is inset with marble footprints marking the starting positions. Pugilists have now been replaced by tourists taking shots of the photogenic San Barnaba **grocery barge** moored at the foot of the bridge.

The huge, damp-ridden San Barnaba church (Mon–Sat 9.30am–12.30pm), built in 1749, has a trompe-l'oeil ceiling painting of *St Barnabas in Glory* by Constantino Cedini, a follower of Tiepolo. Despite recent restoration, the ceiling is being restored again because of moisture damage.

Ca' Rezzonico

April–Oct 10am–6pm; Nov–March 10am–5pm; closed Tues. €6.50.

The **Museo del Settecento Veneziano** – The Museum of the Venetian Eighteenth Century – spreads through most of the enormous Ca' Rezzonico, a palazzo which the city authorities bought in 1934 specifically as a home for the museum. It has never been one of the most popular of Venice's museums, but a recently completed renovation might go some way to rectifying its unjustified neglect.

A man in constant demand in the early part of the eighteenth century was the Belluno sculptor-cum-woodcarver **Andrea Brustolon**, much of whose output consisted of wildly elaborate pieces of furniture, exemplified by the stuff on show in the Brustolon Room. The less fervid imaginations of **Giambattista Tiepolo** and his son **Giandomenico** are

▼ CA' REZZONICO

introduced in room 2 with the ceiling fresco celebrating Ludovico Rezzonico's marriage into the hugely powerful Savorgnan family in 1758. Beyond room 4, with its array of pastels by **Rosalba Carriera**, you come to two other Tiepolo ceilings, enlivening the rooms overlooking the Canal Grande on each side of the main portego: an *Allegory of Merit* by Giambattista and Giandomenico, and *Nobility and Virtue Triumphing over Perfidy*, a solo effort by the father.

▲ CA' MACANA

In the portego of the second floor hang the only two canal views by **Canaletto** on show in public galleries in Venice. The next suite of rooms contains the museum's most engaging paintings – Giandomenico Tiepolo's sequence of **frescoes from the Villa Zianigo** near Mestre, the Tiepolo family home. There then follows a succession of rooms with delightful portraits and depictions of everyday Venetian life by **Francesco Guardi** (including high-society recreation in the parlour of San Zaccaria's convent) and **Pietro Longhi**, whose artlessly candid work – such as a version of the famous *Rhinoceros* – has more than enough curiosity value to make up for its shortcomings in execution.

The low-ceilinged rooms of the third and fourth floor contain the Pinacoteca Egidio Martini, a large but rarely thrilling private donation of Venetian art from the fifteenth to twentieth centuries, but you do get a tremendous view across the rooftops from here, and there's one unusual exhibit: an old **pharmacy**, comprising a sequence of wood-panelled rooms heavily stocked with ceramic jars and glass bottles. Back on the ground floor, steps lead up to the Mestrovich collection, which is considerably smaller and less engrossing than the Martini bequest.

Shops

Ca' Macana
Calle delle Botteghe 3172 @www .camacana.com. Daily 10am–6pm. Huge mask shop, with perhaps the biggest stock in the city; has another branch on the other side of Campo S. Barnaba, at Barbaria delle Tole 1169.

Il Grifone
Fondamenta del Gaffaro 3516. Tues–Sat 10am–1pm & 4–7.30pm. Handmade briefcases, satchels, purses and other sturdy leather pieces, at decent prices.

La Nave d'Oro
Campo S. Margherita 3664. Mon 5–8pm, Tues–Sat 8.30am–1.30pm & 5–8.30pm. This is the city's best outlet for local wines, selling not just bottles but also draught Veneto wines to take out. Other branches are at: Calle del Mondo Novo, Castello 5786; Rio Terrà S. Leonardo, Cannaregio 1370; and Via Lépanto, Lido 241.

Libreria della Toletta

Sacca della Toletta 1214. July & Aug Mon–Sat 9.30am–1pm & 3.30–7.30pm; rest of year Mon–Sat 9.30am–7.30pm, Sun 3.30–7.30pm. Sells reduced-price books, mainly in Italian, but some dual language and translations. Two adjacent branches sell art, design, architecture and photography titles, including bargains on Electa books.

MondoNovo

Rio Terrà Canal 3063 ⓦ www .mondonovomaschere.it. Mon–Sat 9am–6.30pm. This mask workshop, located just off Campo S. Margherita, is perhaps the most imaginative in the city, producing everything from ancient Greek tragic masks to portraits of Richard Wagner.

Cafés, pasticcerie and gelaterie

Causin

Campo S. Margherita 2996. Closed Sun. The ice cream created by Davide Causin rates among the best in all of Italy, and each year he adds a new flavour to his repertoire – such as *manna*, derived from the sap of ash trees. His café has seating on the campo.

Il Caffè

Campo S. Margherita 2963. Mon–Sat 8am–2am. Known as *Caffè Rosso* for its big red sign, this small, atmospheric, old-fashioned café-bar is a big student favourite.

Il Doge

Campo S. Margherita 3058. Open daily till midnight, until 2am June–Sept. Closed Nov & Dec. Well-established *gelateria*. Like *Causin*, it ranks among the city's best.

Nico

Zàttere ai Gesuati 922. Closed Thurs. This café is celebrated for an artery-clogging creation called a *gianduiotto* – ask for one *da passeggio* (to take out) and you'll be given a paper cup with a block of praline ice cream drowned in whipped cream.

Tonolo

Crosera S. Pantalon 3764. Closed Mon. One of the busiest cafés on one of the busiest streets of the student district; especially hectic on Sunday mornings, when the

▼ NICO

fancy *Tonolo* cakes are in high demand.

Restaurants

Ae Oche

Zàttere Ponte Lungo 1414 ☎041.520.6601. Open daily noon–3pm & 7pm–midnight (1am Fri & Sat). Sibling of the *Ae Oche* near San Giacomo (see p.105), this is essentially a huge pizzeria, with a big dining room and waterfront tables too; it does a few other basic dishes, but the huge repertoire of pizzas is what people come for.

Ai Quattro Ferri

Calle Lunga S. Barnaba 2754/a ☎041.520.6978. Closed Sun. Popular and very highly recommended *osteria* just off Campo S. Barnaba with a menu that changes daily but often consists entirely of fish and seafood. No credit cards. Booking essential in high season.

Casin dei Nobili

Calle Lombardo 2765 ☎041.241.1841. Closed Mon. Popular with both locals and tourists, this place serves excellent pizzas (from 7pm) plus a varied menu that includes local specialities such as fish. *Casin* or *casino* means brothel, as you'll gather from the place mats – not to be confused with *casinò*, which means casino.

Da Gianni

Zàttere ai Gesuati 918a. Closed Wed. Nicely sited restaurant-pizzeria, right by the Zàttere vaporetto stop; some rate the pizzas as the best in Venice.

La Bitta

Calle Lunga S. Barnaba 2753a

☎041.523.0531. Mon–Sat 6.30–11pm. No credit cards. Innovative fare on a menu that's remarkable for featuring no fish. Marcellino runs the kitchen while his wife Debora serves and cajoles the guests, offering expert guidance on the impressive wine and grappa list. Delicious cheese platter, served with honey and fruit chutney. Tiny dining room (and garden), so booking is essential.

La Piscina

Zàttere ai Gesuati 780 ☎041.520.6466. Closed Mon. Stretching onto the waterfront outside the *Calcina* hotel, to which it's attached, this is one of the most enjoyable restaurants in Dorsoduro. The service is excellent, the menu of salads and light Mediterranean dishes sets it apart from its neighbours, and the view of Giudecca from the terrace is wonderful.

L'Avogaria

Calle dell'Avogaria 1629 ☎041.296.0491. Closed Tues. The ultra-refined *Avogaria* styles itself as a lounge, restaurant, café and style shop, which gives you an idea of its self-image. The presence of *orrechiette* (thick little pasta "ears") on the menu is a clue to the Puglian origins of the proprietors, who give a distinctive twist to Venetian seafood – this must be the only restaurant in town that marinades its prawns in grappa.

Bars and snacks

Ai do Draghi

Campo S. Margherita 3665. Open 8am–2am daily. Taking its name from the two dragons on the wall opposite, this is a tiny, friendly café-bar, with a good range of wines. The back room exhibits the work of local photographers and artists.

Café Noir
Crosera S. Pantalon 3805. Open Mon–Sat 7am–2am, Sun 9am–2am.
This is another favourite student bar, with a cosmopolitan all-day crowd chatting over a *spritz* or coffee. The neighbouring *Café Blue* has a similar following.

Cantina del Vino già Schiavi
Fondamenta Nani 992. Open till 8.30pm, closed Sun.
Great bar and wine shop opposite San Trovaso – do some sampling before you buy. Excellent *cicheti*, too.

Da Còdroma
Fondamenta Briati 2540. Open till midnight, closed Sun.
The kind of place where you could sit for an hour or two with a beer and a book and feel comfortable. Popular with students from the nearby University of Architecture. Occasional poetry readings and live jazz. Good food too.

Margaret DuChamp
Campo S. Margherita 3019. Open till 2am, closed Tues.
The classiest of the campo's bars, with a self-consciously chic ambience.

▲ ORANGE

Orange
Campo S. Margherita 3054a. Mon-Sat 7.30am–2am.
The newest bar on the campo, *Orange* calls itself a "restaurant and champagne lounge", but it's the cocktail list, in-house DJ and the open-air roof terrace (used as a dancefloor in good weather) that have made it a big hit.

Nightlife

Round Midnight
Fondamenta del Squero 3102. Fri & Sat (and some Thursdays) midnight–4am; closed July–Sept.
Free admission ensures that every square centimetre of the tiny dancefloor is packed with students. This is the nearest thing Venice has to a good club.

San Polo and Santa Croce

As far as the day-to-day life of Venice is concerned, the focal points of the San Polo and Santa Croce *sestieri* are the sociable open space of Campo San Polo and the Rialto area, once the commercial heart of the Republic and still the home of a market that's famous far beyond the boundaries of the city. The bustle of the stalls and the unspoilt bars used by the porters are a good antidote to cultural overload. Nobody, however, should miss the extraordinary pair of buildings in the southern part of San Polo: the colossal Gothic church of the Frari, embellished with three of Venice's finest altarpieces, and the Scuola Grande di San Rocco, decorated with an unforgettable cycle of paintings by Tintoretto.

In the northern part of the district, Venice's modern art, oriental and natural history museums are clustered together on the bank of the Canal Grande: the first two collections occupy one of the city's most magnificent palaces, while the third is installed in the former head-quarters of the Turkish merchants. As ever, numerous treasures are also scattered among the minor churches – for example in San Cassiano and San Simeone Grande. Lastly, if you're in search of a spot in which to sit for an hour and just watch the world go by, head for the Campo San Giacomo dell'Orio, one of Venice's more spacious and tranquil squares.

The Rialto

As the political centre of Venice grew around San Marco, the Rialto became the commercial area. In the twelfth century Europe's first state bank was opened here, and the financiers of this quarter were to be the heavyweights of the international currency exchanges for the next three hundred years and more. And through the **markets of the Rialto** Venice earned a reputation as the bazaar of

▼ DELIVERIES AT RIALTO MARKET

Europe. Trading had been going on here for over four hundred years when, in the winter of 1514, a fire destroyed everything in the area except the church. Reconstruction began almost straight away: the **Fabbriche Vecchie di Rialto** (the arcaded buildings along the Ruga degli Orefici and around the Campo San Giacomo) were finished eight years after the fire, with Sansovino's **Fabbriche Nuove di Rialto** (running along the Canal Grande) following about thirty years later.

Today's Rialto market is tamer than that of Venice at its peak, but it's still one of the liveliest spots in the city, and one of the few places where it is possible to stand in a crowd and hear nothing but Italian spoken. You'll find fruit sellers, vegetable stalls, cheese kiosks, a number of good *alimentari* and some fine old-fashioned bars here. In short, if you can't find something to excite your taste buds around the Rialto, they must be in a sorry state. The Rialto market is open Monday to Saturday 8am to 1pm, with a few stalls opening again later in the afternoon; the **Pescheria** (fish market) – of no practical interest to picnickers but a sight not to be missed – is closed on Monday as well.

Venetian legend asserts that the city was founded at noon on Friday, March 25, 421; from the same legend derives the claim that the church of **San Giacomo di Rialto**, or San Giacometto (Mon–Sat 9.30–noon & 4–6pm), was consecrated in that year, and is thus the oldest church in Venice. It might actually be the oldest, though it was rebuilt in 1071. Parts of the present structure date from this period – the

interior's six columns of ancient Greek marble have eleventh-century Veneto-Byzantine capitals – and it seems likely that the reconstruction of the church prompted the establishment of the market here.

On the opposite side of the campo from the church crouches a stone figure known as the **Gobbo di Rialto** or the Rialto hunchback. It supports a granite platform from which state proclamations were read simultaneously with their announcement from the Pietra del Bando, beside San Marco; it had another role as well – certain wrongdoers were sentenced to run the gauntlet, stark naked, from the Piazza to the Gobbo.

San Cassiano

The barn-like church of San Cassiano (daily 9am–noon & 5–7pm) is a building you're bound to pass as you wander out of the Rialto. The thirteenth-century campanile is the only appealing aspect of the exterior, but inside there are three fine paintings by **Tintoretto**: *The Resurrection*, *The Descent into Limbo* and *The Crucifixion*. The third is one of the most startling pictures in Venice – centred on the ladder on which the executioners stand, it is painted as though the observer were lying in the grass at the foot of the Cross.

Campo San Cassiano was the site of the **first public opera house** in the world – it opened in 1636, at the peak of Monteverdi's career. Long into the following century Venice's opera houses were among the most active in Europe; around five hundred works received their first performances here in the first half of the eighteenth century.

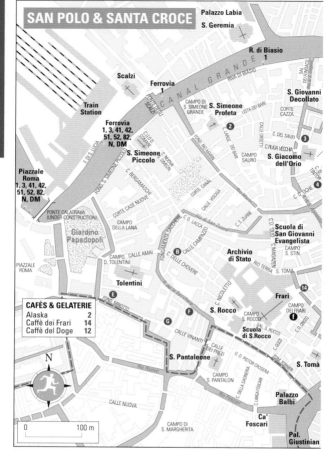

SAN POLO & SANTA CROCE

Palazzo Labia
S. Geremia

R. di Biasio
1

Scalzi
Ferrovia
1

Train
Station

Ferrovia
1, 3, 41, 42,
51, 52, 82,
N, DM

S. Simeone
Piccolo

Piazzale
Roma
1, 3, 41, 42,
51, 52, 82,
N, DM

PIAZZALE
ROMA

PONTE CALATRAVA
(UNDER CONSTRUCTION)

Giardino
Papadopoli

CAMPO
DELLA LANA

CAMPO
D. TOLENTINI

Tolentini

S. Simeone
Profeta

CAMPO DI
S. SIMEONE
GRANDE

S. Giovanni
Decollato

CORTE
CAZZA

S. Giacomo
dell'Orio

CAMPO
SAURO

Scuola di
San Giovanni
Evangelista

CAMPO
S. STIN

Archivio
di Stato

Frari

CAMPO
DEL FRARI

CAFÉS & GELATERIE

Alaska	2
Caffè dei Frari	14
Caffè del Doge	12

S. Rocco

CAMPO
S. ROCCO

Scuola
di S.Rocco

S. Tomà

CALLE VINANTI

S. Pantaleone

CAMPO
S. PANTALON

Palazzo
Balbi

CALLE NUOVA

Ca'
Foscari

Pal.
Giustinian

CAMPO DI
S. MARGHERITA

N

0   100 m

Santa Maria Mater Domini

The small **Campo Santa
Maria Mater Domini**
would have to be included in
any anthology of the hidden
delights of Venice; it is a
typically Venetian miscellany – a
thirteenth-century house (the
Casa Zane), a few ramshackle
Gothic houses, an assortment
of stone reliefs of indeterminate
age, a fourteenth-century well-
head in the centre, a couple

of bars and an ironsmith's
workshop tucked into one
corner. The church of Santa
Maria Mater Domini (Tues–Fri
10am–noon), an early sixteenth-
century building, boasts an
endearing *Martyrdom of St
Christina* by **Vincenzo Catena**.

Ca' Pésaro

The Ca' Pésaro was bequeathed
to the city at the end of the
nineteenth century by the

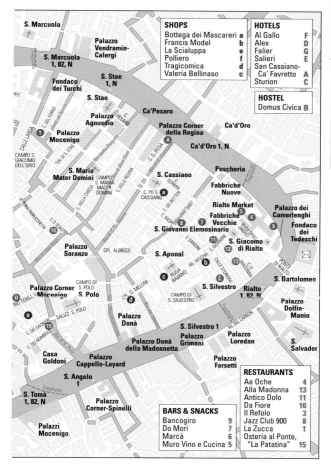

SHOPS		HOTELS	
Bottega dei Mascareri	**a**	Al Gallo	**F**
Francis Model	**b**	Alex	**D**
La Scialuppa	**e**	Falier	**G**
Polliero	**f**	Salieri	**E**
Tragicomica	**d**	San Cassiano–	
Valeria Bellinaso	**c**	Ca' Favretto	**A**
		Sturion	**C**

HOSTEL	
Domus Civica	**B**

RESTAURANTS	
Ae Oche	4
Alla Madonna	13
Antico Dolo	11
Da Fiore	10
Il Refolo	3
Jazz Club 900	8
La Zucca	1
Osteria al Ponte, "La Patatina"	15

BARS & SNACKS	
Bancogiro	9
Do Mori	7
Marcà	6
Muro Vino e Cucina	5

Duchessa Felicità Bevilacqua La Masa, who stipulated in her will that it should provide studio and exhibition space for impoverished young artists. Adventurous shows were staged here for a while, but instead of becoming a permanent centre for the living arts the palazzo has become home to the **Galleria Internazionale d'Arte Moderna** (Tues–Sun: April–Oct 10am–6pm; Nov–March 10am–5pm; €5.50, or Museum Pass/Venice Card). Much of the stuff in this collection is modern only in the chronological sense of the term: pieces bought from the Biennale formed the foundation of the collection, and in its early years the Biennale was far from being a showcase for the avant-garde. Though big names such as Klimt, Kandinsky, Matisse, Klee, Nolde, Ernst and Miró

▲ EXTERIOR OF SAN STAE

San Stae and the Scuola dei Battioro e Tiraoro

Calle Pésaro takes you over the Rio della Rioda to the seventeenth-century church of San Stae (Mon–Sat 10am–5pm, Sun 1–5pm; €2.50, or Chorus Pass). In the chancel there's a series of paintings from the beginning of the eighteenth century, the pick of which are *The Martyrdom of St James the Great* by Piazzetta (low on the left), *The Liberation of St Peter* by Sebastiano Ricci (same row) and *The Martyrdom of St Bartholomew* by Giambattista Tiepolo (opposite). Exhibitions and concerts are often held in San Stae, and exhibitions are also held from time to time in the diminutive building alongside, the early seventeenth-century **Scuola dei Battioro e Tiraoro** (goldsmiths' guild).

Palazzo Mocenigo

Tues–Sun: April–Oct 10am–5pm; Nov–March 10am–4pm. €4, or Museum Pass/Venice Card. Halfway down the alley flanking San Stae is the early seventeenth-century Palazzo Mocenigo, now home to a centre for the study of textiles and clothing. The library and archive of the study centre occupy part of the building, but

are to be found here, this is not one of Europe's first-rank museums. An air of neglect hangs over over the **Museo Orientale**, on the palace's top floor. There are some very fine pieces among the jumble of lacquer work, armour, weaponry and so forth, but the collection is so badly presented (labelling is almost non-existent) that it will make very little sense to the uninitiated.

Who's San Stae?

Among the chief characteristics of the Venetian vernacular are its tendencies to slur consonants and truncate vowels. For example, the Italian name Giuseppe here becomes Isepo, Giuliano becomes Zulian, Eustachio becomes Stae, Biagio becomes Biasio (or Blasio), Agostino shrinks to Stin, and Giovanni is Zuan or Zan – as in San Zan Degolà, for San Giovanni Decollato.

You'll see *dose* instead of *doge*, *do* instead of *due* (two), *nove* instead of *nuove*, *fontego* for *fondaco* and *sestier* for *sestiere*. In Venetian dialect a shop isn't *aperto* (open), it's *verto*. An ice cream is a *geáto*, not a *gelato*.

You'll also notice that the letter 'x' occasionally replaces 'z' (as in venexiana), and that the final vowel is habitually lopped off Venetian surnames, as in Giustinian, Loredan, Vendramin and Corner, to cite just four of the most conspicuous instances.

a substantial portion of the *piano nobile* is open to the public, and there are few Venetian interiors of this date that have been so meticulously preserved. The main room is decorated with workaday portraits of various Mocenigo men, while the rooms to the side are full of miscellaneous pictures, antique furniture, Murano chandeliers and display cases of dandified clothing and cobweb-fine lacework. The curtains are kept closed to protect such delicate items as floral silk stockings, silvery padded waistcoats and an extraordinarily embroidered outfit once worn by what must have been the best-dressed 5-year-old in town.

San Giovanni Decollato

Mon–Sat 10am–noon. The signposted route to the train station passes the deconsecrated church of San Giovanni Decollato, or San Zan Degolà in dialect – it means "St John the Beheaded". Established in the opening years of the eleventh century, it has retained its layout through several alterations; the columns and capitals of the nave date from the first century of its existence, and parts of its fragmentary **frescoes** (at the east end) could be of the same age. Some of the paintings are certainly thirteenth century, and no other church in Venice has frescoes that pre-date them. The church also has one of the city's characteristic ship's-keel ceilings.

The Museo di Storica Naturale

The Museo di Storia Naturale is right by the church, in the **Fondaco dei Turchi**, which was once a hostel-cum-warehouse for Turkish traders. Top-billing exhibits are the remains of a 37-foot-long ancestor of the crocodile and an Ouranosaurus, both dug up in the Sahara in 1973; of stricter relevance to Venetian life is the display relating to the lagoon's marine life, and a pre-Roman boat dredged from the silt. However, for many years the building has been undergoing a major restoration, and at the moment only the aquarium and dinosaur room are open (Tues–Fri 9am–1pm, Sat & Sun 10am–4pm; free).

San Giacomo dell'Orio

Mon–Sat 10am–5pm, Sun 1–5pm. €2.50, or Chorus Pass.
Standing in a lovely campo which, despite its size, you could easily miss if you weren't looking for it, San Giacomo dell'Orio is an ancient and atmospheric church. Founded in the ninth century (the shape of the apse betrays its Byzantine origins), it was rebuilt in 1225 and remodelled on numerous subsequent occasions, notably

▼ SAN GIACOMO DELL'ORIO

when its **ship's-keel roof** was added in the fourteenth century. Several fine paintings are to be seen here. The main altarpiece, *Madonna and Four Saints*, was painted by Lorenzo Lotto in 1546, shortly before he left the city complaining that the Venetians had not treated him fairly; the Crucifix that hangs in the air in front of it is attributed to Paolo Veneziano. In the left transept there's an altarpiece by Paolo Veronese, and there's a fine set of pictures from Veronese's workshop on the ceiling of the **new sacristy**. The **old sacristy** is a showcase for the art of Palma il Giovane, whose cycle in celebration of the Eucharist covers the walls and part of the ceiling.

San Simeone Profeta

Mon–Sat 9am–noon & 5–6.30pm.
San Giacomo dell'Orio is plumb in the middle of an extensive residential district, much of which is as close to bland as you can get in Venice. Don't, though, overlook the church of San Simeone Profeta (or Grande) – remarkable for its reclining **effigy of St Simeon** (to the left of the chancel), a luxuriantly bearded, larger than lifesize figure, whose half-open mouth disturbingly creates the impression of the moment of death. According to its inscription, it was sculpted in 1317 by **Marco Romano**, but some experts doubt that the sculpture can be that old, as nothing else of that date bears comparison with it. Originating in the tenth century, the church has often been rebuilt – most extensively in the eighteenth century, when the city sanitation experts, anxious about the condition of the plague victims who had been buried under the

▲ SAN POLO

flagstones in the 1630 epidemic, ordered the whole floor to be relaid.

San Polo

South of the Rialto, **Ruga Vecchia San Giovanni** constitutes the first leg of the right bank's nearest equivalent to the Mercerie of San Marco, a reasonably straight chain of shop-lined alleyways that is interrupted by **Campo San Polo**, the largest square in Venice after the Piazza. In earlier times it was the site of weekly markets and occasional fairs, as well as being used as a parade ground and bullfighting arena. And on one occasion Campo San Polo was the scene of a bloody act of political retribution: on February 26, 1548, Lorenzaccio de'Medici, having fled Florence after murdering the deranged duke Alessandro (a distant relative and former friend), was murdered here by assassins sent by Duke Cosimo I, Alessandro's successor.

The bleak interior of San Polo church (Mon–Sat 10am–5pm,

Sun 1–5pm; €2.50, or Chorus Pass) is worth a visit for a superior *Last Supper* by Tintoretto (on the left as you enter) and a cycle of the *Stations of the Cross (Via Crucis)* by Giandomenico Tiepolo in the Oratory of the Crucifix, painted when the artist was only 20.

Casa Goldoni

Mon–Sat 10am–5pm, Nov–March closes 4pm. €2.50, or Museum Pass/Venice Card. The fifteenth-century **Palazzo Centani**, in Calle dei Nomboli, was the birthplace of **Carlo Goldoni** (1707–93), the playwright who transformed the *commedia dell'arte* from a vehicle for semi-improvised clowning into a medium for sharp political observation. Goldoni's plays are still the staple of theatrical life in Venice, and there's no risk of running out of material – allegedly, he once bet a friend that he could produce one play a week for a whole year, and won. Goldoni's home now houses a theatre studies institute and the **Museo Goldoni**, a very small collection of first editions, portraits and theatrical paraphernalia, including some eighteenth-century marionettes and a miniature theatre.

Santa Maria Gloriosa dei Frari

Mon–Sat 9am–6pm, Sun 1–6pm. €2.50, or Chorus Pass.

Santa Maria Gloriosa dei Frari – always abbreviated to the **Frari** – was founded by the Franciscans around 1250, not long after the death of their founder, but almost no sooner was the first church completed (in 1338) than work began on a vast replacement, a project which took well over a hundred years. The campanile, one of the city's landmarks and the tallest after San Marco's, was finished in 1396.

You're unlikely to fall in love at first sight with this mountain of brick, but the outside of the church is a misleadingly dull prelude to an astounding interior. Apart from the Accademia and the Salute, the Frari is the only building in Venice with more than a single first-rate work by **Titian**. One of these – the **Assumption** – you'll see right away, as it soars over the high altar; it is a piece of compositional and colouristic bravura for which there was no precedent in Venetian art (no previous altarpiece had emphasized the vertical axis), and the other Titian masterpiece here, the **Madonna di Ca'Pésaro** (on the left wall, between the third

▲ BELLINI'S ALTARPIECE, FRARI

and fourth columns), was equally innovative in its displacement of the figure of the Virgin from the centre of the picture. Other paintings to look out for are Bartolomeo Vivarini's *St Mark Enthroned* (in the Cappella Corner, at the end of the left transept); Alvise Vivarini's *St Ambrose and other Saints* (in the adjoining chapel, where you'll also find the grave of Monteverdi); and, above all, **Giovanni Bellini**'s serene and solemn *Madonna and Child with SS Nicholas of Bari, Peter, Mark and Benedict*, in the **sacristy**.

Apart from its paintings, the Frari is also remarkable for **Donatello**'s luridly naturalistic wooden statue of *St John the Baptist* (in the chapel to the right of the transept), the beautiful fifteenth-century monks' choir and its wealth of extravagant tombs. Two of the finest monuments

▲ TITIAN'S *ASSUMPTION*, THE FRARI

flank the Titian *Assumption*: on the left is the proto-Renaissance **tomb of Doge Niccolò Tron**, by Antonio Rizzo and assistants (1476); on the right, the more archaic and chaotic **tomb of Doge Francesco Fóscari**, carved shortly after Fóscari's

The scuole

The Venetian institutions known as the **scuole** originated in 1260 with the formation of the confraternity called the **Scuola di Santa Maria della Carità**, the first of the so-called **scuole grande**. By the middle of the sixteenth century there were five more of these major confraternities – **San Giovanni Evangelista**, **San Marco**, **Santa Maria della Misericordia**, **San Rocco** and **San Teodoro** – plus scores of smaller bodies known as the **scuole minore**, of which at one time there were as many as four hundred. The *scuole grande*, drawing much of their membership from the wealthiest professional and mercantile groups, and with rosters of up to six hundred men, received subscriptions that allowed them to fund lavish architectural and artistic projects, of which the Scuola Grande di San Rocco is the most spectacular example. The *scuole minore*, united by membership of certain guilds (eg goldsmiths at the Scuola dei Battioro e Tiraoro, or by common nationality (as with San Giorgio degli Schiavoni, the Slavs' *scuola*), generally operated from far more modest bases. Yet all *scuole* had the same basic functions – to provide assistance for their members (eg dowries and medical aid), to offer a place of communal worship and to distribute alms and services in emergencies (anything from plague relief to the provision of troops).

death in 1457 (after 34 years as doge) by Antonio and Paolo Bregno.

Against the right-hand wall of the nave stands the house-sized **monument to Titian**, built in the mid-nineteenth century on the supposed place of his burial. The artist died in 1576, in around his ninetieth year, a casualty of the plague; such was the esteem in which Titian was held, he was the only victim to be allowed a church burial in the course of the outbreak. The marble pyramid on the opposite side of the church is the **Mausoleum of Canova**, erected by pupils of the sculptor, following a design he himself had made for the tombs of Titian and Maria Christina of Austria. Finally, you can't fail to notice what is surely the most grotesque monument in the city, the tomb of **Doge Giovanni Pésaro** (1669), held aloft by gigantic ragged-trousered Moors and decomposing corpses.

The Scuola Grande di San Rocco

Daily: April–Oct 9am–5.30pm; Nov–March 10am–5pm. €5.50.

Unless you've been to the Scuola Grande di San Rocco you can't properly appreciate the achievement of **Tintoretto**. Ruskin called it "one of the three most precious buildings in Italy", and it's not difficult to understand why he resorted to such hyperbole. (His other votes were for the Sistine Chapel and the Campo Santo at Pisa – the latter was virtually ruined in World War II.) The unremitting concentration and restlessness of Tintoretto's paintings won't inspire unqualified enthusiasm in everyone, but even those who prefer their art at a lower voltage should find this an overwhelming experience.

From its foundation in 1478, the special concern of this particular *scuola* was the relief of the sick – a continuation of the Christian mission of its patron saint, **St Roch** (Rocco) of Montpellier, who in 1315 left his home town to work among plague victims in Italy. The Scuola had been going for seven years when the body of the saint was brought to Venice from Germany, and the consequent boom in donations was so great that in 1489 it acquired the status of *scuola grande*. In 1527 the city was hit by an outbreak of plague, and the Scuola's revenue rocketed to record levels as gifts poured in from people hoping to secure St Roch's protection against the disease. The fattened coffers paid for this building, and for **Tintoretto**'s amazing cycle of more than fifty major paintings.

The narrative sequence begins with the first picture in the lower room – the *Annunciation*. But to appreciate Tintoretto's

▼ SCUOLA GRANDE DI SAN ROCCO

development you have to begin in the smaller room on the upper storey – the **Sala dell'Albergo**. This is dominated by the stupendous *Crucifixion* (1565), the most compendious image of the event ever painted. Henry James made even greater claims for it: "Surely no single picture in the world contains more of human life; there is everything in it." Tintoretto's other works here – aside from the *Glorification of St Roch* in the middle of the ceiling (the piece that won him the contract to decorate the whole room) – are on the entrance wall.

Tintoretto finished his contribution to the Sala dell'Albergo in 1567. Eight years later, when the Scuola decided to proceed with the embellishment of the main upper hall – the **chapter house** – he undertook to do the work in return for nothing more than his expenses. In the event he was awarded a lifetime annuity, and then commenced the **ceiling**. The Scuola's governors were so pleased with these three large panels that he was given the task of completing the decoration of

the entire interior. The New Testament scenes around the walls defy every convention of perspective, lighting, colour and even anatomy, a feat of sustained inventiveness that has few equals in Western art. Though he was in his late sixties when he came to paint the **lower hall**, there is no sign of flagging creativity: indeed, the landscapes in the *Flight into Egypt* and the meditative depictions of *St Mary Magdalen* and *St Mary of Egypt* are among the finest he ever created.

The church of San Rocco

Daily 8am–12.30pm & 3–5pm.

Yet more Tintorettos are to be found in the neighbouring church of San Rocco. On the right wall of the nave you'll find *St Roch Taken to Prison*, and below it *The Pool of Bethesda*; only the latter is definitely by Tintoretto. Between the altars on the other side are a couple of good pictures by **Pordenone** – *St Christopher* and *St Martin*. Four large paintings by Tintoretto hang in the chancel, often either lost in the gloom or glazed with sunlight: the best (both painted

▲ GIARDINO PAPADOPOLI

in 1549) are *St Roch Curing the Plague Victims* (lower right) and *St Roch in Prison* (lower left).

The Scuola di San Giovanni Evangelista

Another of the *scuole grandi* nestles in a line of drab buildings very near to the Frari – the Scuola di San Giovanni Evangelista. This institution's finest hour came in 1369, when it was presented with a relic of the True Cross. The miracles effected by the relic were commemorated in a series of paintings by Carpaccio, Gentile Bellini and others, now transplanted to the Accademia. Nowadays the chief attraction of the Scuola is the superb screen of the outer courtyard, built in 1481 by **Pietro Lombardo**. Seen from the train station direction the screen just looks like any old brick wall, but its other face is a wonderfully delicate piece of marble carving.

The Tolentini and the Giardino Papadopoli

Calle della Lacca–Fondamenta Sacchere–Corte Amai is a dullish but uncomplicated route from San Giovanni Evangelista to the portentous church of San Nicolò da Tolentino – alias the Tolentini (daily 8am–noon & 4.30–6.30pm). Among its scores of seventeenth-century **paintings**, two really stand out: a *St Jerome* by Johann Lys, on the wall outside the chancel, to the left; and *St Lawrence Giving Alms* by Bernardo Strozzi, round the corner from the Lys painting. Up the left wall of the chancel swirls the best Baroque monument in Venice: the **tomb of Francesco Morosini**, created in 1678 by a Genoese sculptor, Filippo Parodi.

▲ LA SCIALUPPA

If fatigue is setting in and you need a pit-stop, make for the nearby Giardino Papadopoli, formerly one of Venice's biggest private gardens but now owned by the city.

Shops

Bottega dei Mascareri

Calle del Cristo 2919. Daily 10am–6pm. Run for many years by the brothers Sergio and Massimo Boldrin, the *Bottega dei Mascareri* sells some wonderfully inventive masks, such as faces taken from Tiepolo paintings or Donald Sutherland in Fellini's *Casanova*.

Francis Model

Ruga Rialto 773a. Mon–Sat 9.30am–7.30pm, Sun 10.30am–7.30pm. A father-and-son workshop that produces high-quality handbags and briefcases.

La Scialuppa

Calle Seconda Saoneri 2681 Ⓦ www .veniceboats.com. Mon–Sat 9.30am–12.30pm & 3–6pm.

For a uniquely Venetian gift, call in at Gilberto Penzo's shop, which sells well-priced models, model kits and elegantly drawn plans for Venetian boats.

Polliero

Campo dei Frari 2995. Mon–Sat 10.30am–1pm, Sun 10am–1pm.
A bookbinding workshop that sells patterned paper as well as heavy, leather-bound albums of handmade plain paper.

Rialto market

Mon–Sat approximately 8am–1pm; Pescheria same hours, closed Mon.
The market of markets, where you can buy everything you need for an impromptu feast – wine, cheese (the best stalls in the city are here), fruit, salami, vegetables and bread from nearby bakers or *alimentari* (delicatessens).

Tragicomica

Calle dei Nomboli 2800 ⓦ www.tragicomica.it. Daily 10am–7pm.
A good range of masks and some nice eighteenth-century styles, as you might expect

from a shop that's opposite Goldoni's house.

Valeria Bellinaso

Campo Sant'Aponal 1226. Mon–Fri 10am–1.30pm & 3–7pm, Sat 10am–7pm, Sun 11am–1.30pm & 3–7pm; closed Sun Jan–March, July & Aug.
Delicate silk and velvet shoes, bags, hats and gloves.

Cafés and gelaterie

Alaska

Calle Larga dei Bari 1159. April–Oct open daily; Feb, March & Nov closed Tues. Superb *gelateria*, dishing out adventurous flavours such as artichoke and fennel amid the more traditional concoctions.

Caffè dei Frari

Fondamenta dei Frari 2564. Mon–Sat 8am–9pm. Very pleasant traditional café-bar directly opposite the front door of the Frari.

Caffè del Doge

Calle dei Cinque 609. Daily 7am–7pm.

▼ CAFFÈ DEL DOGE

Fantastically good coffee (they supply many of the city's bars and restaurants), served in a chic minimalist set-up very close to the Rialto Bridge.

Restaurants

Ae Oche

Calle del Tintor 1552 ☎041.524.1161. Daily noon–3pm & 7pm–midnight, until 1am Fri & Sat. Excellent pizzeria on an alley that leads into the south side of Campo S. Giacomo dell'Orio. Has about eighty varieties to choose from, so if this doesn't do you, nothing will; on summer evenings if you're not there by 8pm you may have to queue on the pavement.

Alla Madonna

Calle della Madonna 594. Closed Wed. Roomy, loud and bustling seafood restaurant that's been going strong for four decades. Little finesse but good value for money, and many locals rate its kitchen as one of the city's best, though standards are far from consistent. Reservations not accepted, so be prepared to queue.

Antico Dolo

Ruga Vecchia S. Giovanni 778 ☎041.522.6546. Daily noon–11pm. This excellent long-established *osteria* is a good source of simple meals or bar-food near the Rialto.

Da Fiore

Calle del Scaleter 2202a ☎041.731.308. Closed Sun & Mon. Refined, elegant and expensive restaurant off Campo S. Polo; prides itself on its seafood, regional cheeses, desserts, homemade bread and wine list. Generally considered among the

▲ DA FIORE

very best in Venice, and service is faultless. You can also drop into the tiny front room bar for a glass of high-quality wine.

Il Refolo

Campiello del Piovan 1459 ☎041.524.0016. Closed Nov–March; rest of year closed all Mon and Tues lunch. Run by the son of the owner of the famous *Da Fiore*, this excellent canalside pizzeria fills up the tiny square which fronts the church of San Giacomo dell'Orio. Good for salads as well.

Jazz Club 900

Campiello del Sansoni 900 ☎041.522.6565. Open until midnight or later; closed Mon. Just off Ruga Vecchia S. Giovanni, the dark-panelled *Novecento* serves some of the best pizzas in the city, accompanied by non-stop jazz (live one day a week for most of the year).

La Zucca

Ponte del Megio 1762 ☎041.524.1570. Closed Sun. Long a well-respected restaurant, *La Zucca* was once a vegetarian establishment (its name means "pumpkin") but now goes against the Venetian grain by featuring a lot of meat – chicken, lamb, beef – and curries. The quality remains high, the prices moderate and the canalside setting is nice.

Osteria al Ponte, "La Patatina"

2741a Calle dei Saoneri
℡041.523.7238. Closed Sun.
Bustling *osteria*, serving excellent *cicheti* and other Venetian specialities, with well-priced set menus that change regularly.

Bars and snacks

Bancogiro

Sottoportego del Banco Giro 122. Open Tues–Sun noon–2am.
Very popular small *osteria*, in a splendid location in the midst of the Rialto market. Come here to nurse a glass of fine wine beside the Canal Grande, or nip upstairs to the dining room for a well-priced and well-prepared meal.

Do Mori

Calle Do Mori 429. Mon–Sat 8.30am–8.30pm. Hidden just off Ruga Vecchia S. Giovanni, this is the most authentic old-style Venetian bar in the market area – some would say in the entire city. It's a single narrow room, with no seating, packed every evening with home-bound shopworkers, Rialto porters and locals just out for a stroll. Delicious snacks, great range of wines, terrific atmosphere.

Marcà

Campo Cesare Battisti 213. Mon–Sat 7am–3pm & 6–9.30pm.
This minuscule stand-up Rialto bar is perfect for a quick *panino* and *prosecco*.

Muro Vino e Cucina

Campo Cesare Battisti 222. Open Mon–Sat till 1am. This slick American-run operation serves good food (the evening menu is expensive, but the set lunch is excellent value), though most of the customers are here for a drink, either in the stylish bar or at one of the outside tables.

Cannaregio

Don't be put off by the hustle around the train station – in Cannaregio it's very easy to get well away from the tourist crowds. The pleasures of this sestiere are generally more a matter of atmosphere than of specific sights, but you shouldn't leave Venice without seeing the Ghetto, the first area in the world to bear that name. There are some special buildings to visit too: Madonna dell'Orto, with its astonishing Tintoretto paintings; Sant'Alvise and the Palazzo Labia, both remarkable for work by Giambattista Tiepolo; the Ca' d'Oro, a gorgeous Canal Grande palace housing a sizeable art collection; the much-loved and highly photogenic Santa Maria dei Miracoli; and the Gesuiti, a Baroque creation which boasts perhaps the weirdest interior in the city.

The Scalzi

Daily 7–11.50am & 4–6.50pm.

Right by the station stands the Scalzi (formally Santa Maria di Nazaretta), which was begun in 1672 for the barefoot ("scalzi") order of Carmelites, but is anything but barefoot itself – the opulent interior is plated with dark, multicoloured marble and overgrown with Baroque statuary. Before an Austrian bomb plummeted through the roof in 1915 (the train station was its intended target) there was a splendid **Giambattista**

Tiepolo ceiling here; a few scraps are preserved in the Accademia, and some wan frescoes by Tiepolo survive in the first chapel on the left and the second on the right. The second chapel on the left is the resting place of **Lodovico Manin** (d.1802), Venice's last doge.

San Geremia

Mon–Sat 8am–noon & 3.30–6.30pm, Sun 9.15am–12.15pm & 5.30–6.30pm.

The church of San Geremia, at the end of the tawdry Lista di

▼ PALAZZIO LABIA AND SAN GEREMIA

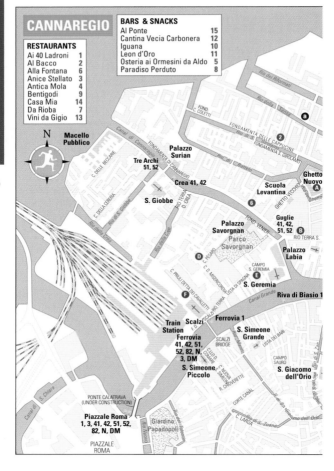

CANNAREGIO

RESTAURANTS

Ai 40 Ladroni	1
Al Bacco	2
Alla Fontana	6
Anice Stellato	3
Antica Mola	4
Bentigodi	9
Casa Mia	14
Da Rioba	7
Vini da Gigio	13

BARS & SNACKS

Al Ponte	15
Cantina Vecia Carbonera	12
Iguana	10
Leon d'Oro	11
Osteria ai Ormesini da Aldo	5
Paradiso Perduto	8

Spagna, is where the travels of **St Lucy** eventually terminated; martyred in Syracuse in 304, she was stolen from Constantinople by Venetian Crusaders in 1204, then ousted from her own church in Venice in the mid-nineteenth century, when it was demolished to make way for the train station. Her desiccated body, wearing a lustrous silver mask, lies behind the altar, reclining above a donations box that bears the prayer "St Lucy, protect my eyes" – she's the patron saint of eyesight (and artists). Nothing else about the church is of interest, except the twelfth-century **campanile**, one of the oldest left in the city.

Palazzo Labia

The Palazzo Labia, next door to San Geremia, was built in 1720–50 for a famously extravagant Catalan family by

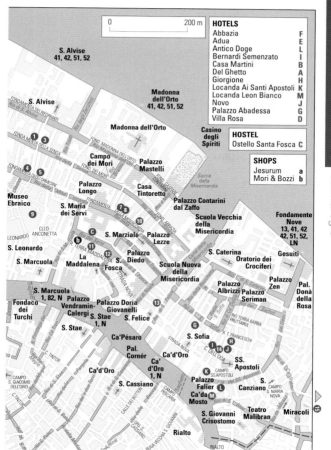

HOTELS

Abbazia	F
Adua	E
Antico Doge	L
Bernardi Semenzato	I
Casa Martini	B
Del Ghetto	A
Giorgione	H
Locanda Ai Santi Apostoli	K
Locanda Leon Bianco	M
Novo	J
Palazzo Abadessa	G
Villa Rosa	D

HOSTEL

Ostello Santa Fosca C

SHOPS

Jesurum	a
Mori & Bozzi	b

the name of Lasbias. No sooner was the interior completed than **Giambattista Tiepolo** was hired to cover the walls of the ballroom with **frescoes** depicting the story of Anthony and Cleopatra. Restored to something approaching its original freshness after years of neglect, this is the only sequence of Tiepolo paintings in Venice that is comparable to his narrative masterpieces in

mainland villas such as the Villa Valmarana near Vicenza. RAI, the Italian state broadcasting company, now owns the palace, but they allow visitors in for a few hours each week (usually Wed, Thurs & Fri 3–4pm; free).

San Giobbe

Mon–Sat 10am–5pm, Sun 1–5pm. €2.50, or Chorus Pass. The Palazzo Labia's longest facade overlooks the **Canale di Cannaregio**, the main entrance to Venice before the rail and road links were constructed; if you turn left immediately before or after the Ponte delle Guglie, you'll reach the Ponte dei Tre Archi (Venice's only multiple-span bridge), where a left turn takes you to the church of San Giobbe. Dedicated to Job, whose sufferings greatly endeared him to the Venetians (who were regularly afflicted with malaria, plague and a plethora of water-related diseases), the church is interesting mainly for its exquisitely carved doorway and chancel – the first Venetian projects of **Pietro Lombardo**. The tomb supported by ludicrous marble beasts is the resting place of the magnificently named Renato de Voyer de Palmy Signore d'Argeson, who served as French ambassador to Venice. The best paintings – a fine triptych by Antonio Vivarini and a *Marriage of St Catherine* attributed to Andrea Previtali – are in the **sacristy**, along with fifteenth-century terracotta bust of the great preacher St Bernardine, who in 1443 was a guest here (in what turned out to be the last year of his life) and whose canonization in 1450 was marked by the rebuilding of this church.

The Ghetto

The name of the Venetian Ghetto – a name bequeathed to all other such enclaves of oppression – is probably derived from the Venetian dialect *geto*, foundry, which

is what this area used to be. The creation of the Ghetto was a consequence of the War of the League of Cambrai, when hundreds of Jews fled the mainland in fear of the Imperial army. Gaining safe haven in Venice, many of the fugitives donated funds for the defence of the city, and were rewarded with permanent protection – at a price. In 1516 the **Ghetto Nuovo** became Venice's Jewish quarter, when all the city's Jews were forced to move onto this small island in the north of Cannaregio. At night the Ghetto was sealed by gates, yet Venice was markedly liberal by the standards of the time, and the Ghetto's population was often swelled by refugees from less tolerant societies – indeed, the Jewish population soon spread into the **Ghetto Vecchio** and the **Ghetto Nuovissimo**. (The adjectives attached to the three parts of the ghetto can be confusing. The Ghetto Nuovo is *nuovo* – new

▼ THE GHETTO

– because the foundries spread here from the Ghetto Vecchio – the old foundry. The Ghetto Nuovissimo, on the other hand, is "most new" because it was the last part to be settled by the city's Jews.) The gates of the Ghetto were finally torn down by Napoleon in 1797, but it wasn't until the unification of Italy that Jews achieved equal status with their fellow citizens.

Each wave of Jewish immigrants maintained their own synagogues with their distinctive rites: the **Scola Tedesca** (for German Jews) was founded in 1528, the **Scola al Canton** (probably Jews from Provence) in 1531–32, the **Scola Levantina** (eastern Mediterranean) in 1538, the **Scola Spagnola** (Spanish) at an uncertain date in the later sixteenth century and the **Scola Italiana** in 1575. Funded by particularly prosperous trading communities, the Scola Levantina and the Scola Spagnola are the most lavish of the synagogues, and are the only two still used on a daily basis.

Depending on the season, one of the above can be viewed, along with the Scola al Canton and the Scola Italiana, in an informative English-language guided tour that begins in the **Museo Ebraico**, above the Scola Tedesca (daily except Sat & Jewish hols: June–Sept 10am–7pm; Oct–May 10am–5.30pm; €3, or free with tour, which costs €8.50; tours in English on the half-hour, last tour June–Sept 5.30pm, Oct–May 4.30pm). The museum's collection consists mainly of silverware, sacred objects, textiles and furniture.

In a corner of the campo is a reminder of the ultimate suffering of the Jewish people: a series of seven **reliefs** by Arbit Blatas commemorating the two hundred Venetian Jews deported to the Nazi death camps; the names and ages of all the victims are inscribed on a separate memorial nearby, entitled *The Last Train*.

Sant'Alvise

Mon–Sat 10am–5pm, Sun 1–5pm. €2.50, or Chorus Pass. Located on the northern periphery of the city, the church of **Sant'Alvise** is notoriously prone to damp, but restoration has refreshed the chancel's immense *Road to Calvary* by Giambattista Tiepolo. His *Crown of Thorns* and *Flagellation*, slightly earlier works, hang on the right-hand wall of the nave. Under the nuns' choir you'll find eight small paintings, known as "The Baby Carpaccios" since Ruskin assigned them to the painter's precocious childhood; they're not actually by Carpaccio, but they were produced around 1470, when he would indeed have been just an infant. "Alvise", by the way, is the Venetian version of Louis/Luigi – the church is dedicated to St Louis of Toulouse.

Campo dei Mori

To get from Sant'Alvise to Madonna dell'Orto you can either take a one-stop vaporetto trip, or cross over the canal to the Fondamenta della Sensa, the main street immediately to the south. Going this way you'll pass the Campo dei Mori, a tiny square whose name may come from the four thirteenth-century **statues** around the campo. They are popularly associated with a family of merchants called the Mastelli brothers, who used to live in the palace into which two of the figures are embedded

▲ SIOR ANTONIO RIOBA, CAMPO DE MORI

– they hailed from the Morea (the Peloponnese), and hence were known as *Mori*. Venice's more malicious citizens used to leave denunciations at the feet of "Sior Antonio Rioba" (the statue with the rusty nose), and circulate vindictive verses signed with his name.

Madonna dell'Orto

Mon–Sat 10am–5pm, Sun 1–5pm. €2.50, or Chorus Pass.

Madonna dell'Orto, the Tintoretto family's parish church, is arguably the finest Gothic church in Venice. Founded in the name of St Christopher some time around 1350, it was popularly renamed after a large stone *Madonna* by **Giovanni de'Santi**, found in a nearby vegetable garden (*orto*), began working miracles; brought into the church in 1377, the heavily restored figure now sits in the Cappella di San Mauro (at the end of the right aisle).

Outside, the church is notable for its statue of *St Christopher*, its elegant portal and its **campanile**, one of the most notable landmarks when approaching Venice from the northern lagoon. Inside, paintings by **Tintoretto** make a massive impact, none more so than the epic picures on each side of the choir: *The Last Judgement* and *The Making of the Golden Calf*. Other Tintorettos adorn the chancel, but none is a match for the tender *Presentation of the Virgin*, at the end of right aisle, which makes a fascinating comparison with Titian's Accademia version of the incident. A major figure of the early Venetian Renaissance, **Cima da Conegliano** – is represented by a *St John the Baptist and Other Saints*, on the first altar on the right; a *Madonna and Child* by Cima's great contemporary, Giovanni Bellini, used to occupy the first chapel on the left, but thieves made off with it in 1993.

Strada Nova

The main land route between the train station and the Rialto Bridge was created in the 1870s by the Austrians. But whereas the Lista di Spagna and Rio Terrà San Leonardo were formed by filling canals with earth, the Strada Nova was created by simply ploughing a line straight through the houses that used to stand there. Outside the church of **Santa Fosca**, at the start of Strada Nova, stands a statue of a true Venetian hero, **Fra' Paolo Sarpi**. A brilliant scholar and scientist (he assisted Galileo's researches), Sarpi was the adviser to the Venetian state in its row with the Vatican at the start of the seventeenth century, when the whole city was excommunicated for its refusal to accept papal jurisdiction in secular affairs. One night Sarpi was walking home past Santa Fosca when he was set upon by three men and left for dead with a dagger in his face. "I recognize the style of the Holy See," Sarpi quipped, punning on the word "stiletto". He survived.

Across the Strada Nova, the **Farmacia Ponci** has the oldest surviving shop interior in Venice, a wonderful display of seventeenth-century heavy-duty woodwork in walnut, kitted out with eighteenth-century majolica vases.

Ca' d'Oro

Mon 8.15am–2pm, Tues–Sat 8.15am–7.15pm. €5. An inconspicuous calle leads down to the Ca' d'Oro (House of Gold), the showpiece of domestic Gothic architecture in Venice and home of the **Galleria Giorgio Franchetti**. The gallery's main attraction is undoubtedly the *St Sebastian* painted by **Mantegna** shortly before his death in 1506, now installed in a chapel-like alcove on the first floor. Many of the big names of Venetian art are found on the second floor, but the canvases by Titian and Tintoretto are not among their best, and Pordenone's fragmentary frescoes from

Santo Stefano require a considerable feat of imaginative reconstruction, as do the remains of Giorgione and Titian's work from the Fondaco dei Tedeschi (see p.37).

The Ca' d'Oro's collection of sculpture, though far less extensive than the array of paintings, has more outstanding items, notably **Tullio Lombardo**'s beautifully carved *Young Couple*, and superb portrait busts by Bernini and Alessandro Vittoria. Also arresting are a sixteenth-century English alabaster polyptych of *Scenes from the Life of St Catherine* and a case of Renaissance medals that includes fine specimens by **Gentile Bellini** and **Pisanello**.

Santi Apostoli

Daily 7.30–11.30am & 5–7pm. At the eastern end of the Strada you come to the Campo dei Santi Apostoli, an elbow on the road from the Rialto to the train station. The most interesting part of Santi Apostoli church is the **Cappella Corner**, off the right side, where the altarpiece is the *Communion of St Lucy* by

▲ MADONNA DELL'ORTO

Giambattista Tiepolo. One of the inscriptions in the chapel is to Caterina Cornaro, who was buried here before being moved to San Salvatore; the tomb of her father Marco (on the right) is probably by Tullio Lombardo, who also carved the peculiar plaque of St Sebastian in the chapel to the right of the chancel.

San Giovanni Crisostomo

Mon–Sat 8.15am–12.15pm & 3–7pm, Sun 3–7pm. In the southernmost corner of Cannaregio stands San Giovanni Crisostomo (John the Golden-Mouthed), named after the eloquent archbishop of Constantinople. It was possibly the last project of Mauro Codussi, and possesses two outstanding altarpieces: in the chapel to the right hangs one of the last works by **Giovanni Bellini**, *SS Jerome, Christopher and Louis of Toulouse*, painted in 1513 when the artist was in his eighties; and on the high altar, **Sebastiano del Piombo**'s gracefully heavy *St John Chrysostom with SS John the Baptist, Liberale, Mary Magdalen, Agnes and Catherine*, painted in 1509–11.

Teatro Malibran

Behind San Giovanni Crisostomo is the Teatro Malibran, which opened in the seventeenth century, was rebuilt in the 1790s and soon after renamed in honour of the great soprano **Maria Malibran** (1808–36), who saved the theatre from bankruptcy by giving a fund-raising recital here. Quite recently unveiled following a protracted restoration, the Malibran is one of the city's chief venues for classical music. The Byzantine arches on the facade of the theatre are said to have once been part of the house of **Marco Polo**'s family, who probably lived in the heavily restored place overlooking the canal at the back of the Malibran, visible from the Ponte Marco Polo.

Santa Maria dei Miracoli

Mon–Sat 10am–5pm, Sun 1–5pm. €2.50, or Chorus Pass. A hop north of here stands the marble-clad church of Santa Maria dei Miracoli, usually known simply by the last word of its name. It was built in 1481–89 to house an image of the Madonna that was credited with the revival of a man who'd spent half an hour at the bottom of the Giudecca canal and of a woman left for dead after being stabbed. Financed by gifts left at the painting's nearby shrine, the church was most likely designed by **Pietro Lombardo**; certainly he and his two sons Tullio and Antonio oversaw the construction, and the three of them executed much of the exquisite carving both inside and out. The miracle-working Madonna still occupies the altar.

The Gesuiti

Daily 10am–noon & 4–6pm.

▲ CA' D'ORO

▲ SANTA MARIA DEI MIRACOLI

The major monument in the northeastern corner of Cannaregio is **Santa Maria Assunta**, commonly known simply as the Gesuiti. Built for the Jesuits in 1714–29, six decades after the foundation here of their first monastery in Venice, the church was clearly planned to make an impression on a city that was habitually mistrustful of the order's close relationship with the papacy. Although the disproportionately huge facade clearly wasn't the work of a weekend, most of the effort went into the stupefying **interior**, where green and white marble covers every wall and stone is carved to resemble swags of damask. The only painting to seek out is the *Martyrdom of St Lawrence* on the first altar on the left, which was painted by **Titian** in 1558.

Oratorio dei Crociferi
Fri & Sat: April–June, Sept & Oct 3–6pm; July & Aug 3.30–6.30pm. €2.
Almost opposite the Gesuiti stands the Oratorio dei Crociferi, the remnant of a convent complex founded in the twelfth century by the crusading religious order known as the *Crociferi* or the Bearers of the Cross. A part of the complex was given over to a hospice for poor women, who were required to help in the maintenance of the convent and to pray each morning in the oratory, which in the 1580s was decorated by **Palma il Giovane** with an impressive cycle of *Scenes from the History of the Order of the Crociferi*.

The Fondamente Nove
The long waterfront to the north of the Gesuiti, the Fondamente Nove (or Nuove), is the chief departure point for **vaporetti** to San Michele, Murano and the northern lagoon. On a clear day you can follow their course as far as the distant island of Burano, and you might even be treated to the startling sight of the snowy Dolomite peaks, apparently hanging in the sky over the Veneto.

Shops

Jesurum
Fondamenta della Sensa 3219. Tues–Sat 10am–1pm & 1.30–5pm.
Renowned for its exquisite lace, *Jesurum* also produces luxurious (and expensive) bed linen, towels and fabrics, all on sale from this factory outlet.

Mori & Bozzi
Rio Terrà della Maddalena 2367. Mon–Sat 9.30am–7.30pm, plus Sun in April, May & Aug–Oct.
The trendiest women's shoe shop in town – no big names, but cool designs at moderate prices.

Restaurants

Ai 40 Ladroni

Fondamenta della Sensa 3253
☎041.715 736. Tues–Sun 10am–
midnight. A new and very busy
osteria, with high-quality *cicheti*
at the bar and similarly good
Venetian standards served at the
tables.

Al Bacco

Fondamenta delle Cappuccine 3054
☎041.717.493. Closed Mon.
Like the *Antica Mola*, farther
east along the canal, *Al
Bacco* started life as a humble
neighbourhood stop-off, but
has grown into a fully fledged
restaurant, with prices to match.
It retains a rough-and-ready
feel, but the food is distinctly
classy.

Alla Fontana

Fondamenta Cannaregio 1102
☎041.715.077. Mon–Sat 6.30–11pm,
closes 10pm in winter.
Once primarily a bar, *Alla
Fontana* has tranformed itself
into an extremely good
trattoria, offering a small and
ever-changing menu of classic
Venetian maritime dishes, often
featuring eel.

▲ ANICE STELLATO

Anice Stellato

Fondamenta della Sensa 3272
☎041.720.744. Closed Mon & Tues.
Hugely popular with Venetians
for the superb, reasonably
priced meals and unfussy
atmosphere. Situated by one of
the northernmost Cannaregio
canals, it's rather too remote for
most tourists. If you can't get
a table – it's frequently booked
solid – at least drop by for the
excellent *cicheti* at the bar.

Antica Mola

Fondamenta degli Ormesini 2800
☎041.710.768. Closed Wed.
This family-run *trattoria*, near
the Ghetto, has become very
popular with tourists, but the
food remains very good value.
There's a nice garden at the back
and canalside tables out front.

Bentigodi

Calle Sele 1423 ☎041.716.269. Daily
10am–3pm & 6pm–1am.
Friendly modern *osteria* just
outside the Ghetto, serving
Venetian dishes in notably
generous portions, backed up
by an extensive wine list. Good
cicheti at the bar. No credit cards.

Casa Mia

Calle dell'Oca 4430 ☎041.528.5590.
Closed Tues. Always heaving with
locals, who usually go for the
pizza list rather than the à la
carte menu, though the standard
dishes are reliable enough.

Da Rioba

Fondamenta della Misericordia 2553
☎041.524.4379. Closed Mon.
This smartly austere and quite
upmarket *osteria* is another
excellent eatery; often full to
bursting, especially in summer,
when tables are set beside the
canal – but the management
always keep the atmosphere
relaxed.

Vini da Gigio
Fondamenta S. Felice 3628a
☎041.528.5140. Closed Mon.
Popular, family-run
wine bar-*trattoria*. It's
now on the tourist
map yet it retains its
authenticity and is still,
by Venetian standards,
excellent value, even if
prices have crept up in
recent years.

▲ CANTINA VECIA CARBONERA

Bars and snacks

Al Ponte
Calle Larga G. Gallina 6378. Open till
8.30pm, closed Sun.
Typical *osteria* just off Campo
Santi Giovanni e Paolo. Good
for a glass of wine and a snack.

Cantina Vecia Carbonera
Rio Terrà della Maddalena 2329. Open
till 11pm most nights; closed Mon.
Old-style *bacarò* atmosphere
and chilled-out playlist attract
a young, stylish clientele. Good
wine, excellent snacks and
plenty of space to sit down.

Iguana
Fondamenta della Misericordia 2517.
Open Tues–Sun till 2am, happy hour
6–8pm.
This cross between a *bacarò*
and a Mexican cantina serves
reasonably priced Mexican fare
to a young crowd. Live music
(Latin, rock and jazz) Tues
9–11pm and some weekends.

Leon d'Oro
Rio Terrà della Maddalena 2345. Open
until 12.30am. Closed Wed.
A pleasant family-run place,
offering sandwiches, with *osteria*
food at the back.

Osteria ai Ormesini da Aldo
Fondamenta degli Ormesini 2710. Open
Mon–Sat till 2am.

One of a number of bars
beside this long canal, and a
particularly pleasant spot for a
lunchtime snack in the sun.

Paradiso Perduto
Fondamenta della Misericordia 2540.
Open daily 7pm–1am, plus Fri–Sun
11am–3pm. Though it serves
food (not inexpensive and
often not good) at its refectory-
like tables, *Paradiso Perduto* is
essentially Venice's leading boho
bar, run by the indefatigable
trumpet-playing Maurizio. Live
music – blues, jazz or whatever
– usually on Sun, sometimes
Mon, until 11pm.

Opera and classical music

Teatro Malibran
Corte Milion 5873 Along with the
Fenice, this is the city's main
venue for big-name classical
concerts, but it also hosts the
occasional big-name jazz gig
and Italian rockers such as
Ligabue. Tickets tend to start
around €20 (discounts for
under-30s) and can be bought
from the same outlets as for
the Fenice (see p.77). The
Malibran ticket office sells
tickets only on the night of the
concert, from around one hour
before the start.

Central Castello

Bordering San Marco on one side and spreading across the city from Cannaregio in the west to the housing estates of Sant'Elena in the east, Castello is so unwieldy a *sestiere* that we've cut it in two for the purposes of this guide. This chapter starts off at its western border and stops in the east at a line drawn north from the landmark Pietà church; the atmospherically distinct area beyond this boundary is covered in the next chapter. The points of interest in this area are evenly distributed, but in terms of its importance and its geographical location, Castello's central building is the immense Gothic church of Santi Giovanni e Paolo (or Zanipolo), the pantheon of Venice's doges. The museums lie in the southern zone – the Querini-Stampalia picture collection, the museum at San Giorgio dei Greci, and the Museo Diocesano's sacred art collection. This southern area's dominant building is the majestic San Zaccaria, right by the southern waterfront and Venice's main promenade, the Riva degli Schiavoni.

Santi Giovanni e Paolo

Mon–Sat 7.30am–7pm, Sun 7.30am–6pm. €2.50. Like the Frari, the massive Gothic brick edifice of Santi Giovanni e Paolo – slurred by the Venetian dialect into **San Zanipolo** – was built for one of the mendicant orders, whose social mission (preaching to and tending the sick and the poor) required a lot of space for their congregrations. The first church built on this site was begun in 1246 after Doge Giacomo Tiepolo (d. 1249) was inspired by a dream to donate the land to the Dominicans. Tiepolo's simple sarcophagus is outside, on the left of the door, next to that of his son Doge Lorenzo Tiepolo (d.1275); the cavernous interior – approximately 90

▼ SANTI GIOVANNI E PAOLO

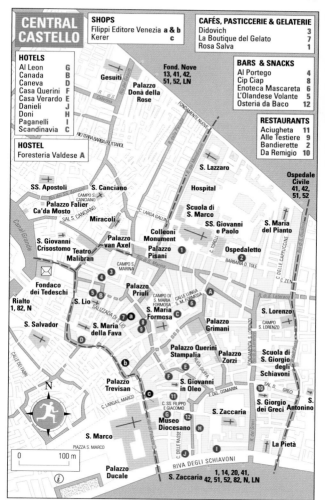

CENTRAL CASTELLO

SHOPS
Filippi Editore Venezia **a & b**
Kerer **c**

CAFÉS, PASTICCERIE & GELATERIE
Didovich 3
La Boutique del Gelato 7
Rosa Salva 1

HOTELS
Al Leon **G**
Canada **B**
Caneva **D**
Casa Querini **F**
Casa Verardo **E**
Danieli **J**
Doni **H**
Paganelli **I**
Scandinavia **C**

HOSTEL
Foresteria Valdese **A**

BARS & SNACKS
Al Portego 4
Cip Ciap 8
Enoteca Mascareta 6
L'Olandese Volante 5
Osteria da Baco 12

RESTAURANTS
Aciugheta 11
Alle Testiere 9
Bandierette 2
Da Remigio 10

Map labels: Fond. Nove 13, 41, 42, 51, 52, LN · Gesuiti · Palazzo Donà della Rose · S. Lazzaro · Ospedale Civile 41, 42, 51, 52 · SS. Apostoli · S. Canciano · Hospital · Palazzo Falier Ca'da Mosto · Scuola di S. Marco · S. Maria del Pianto · Miracoli · SS. Giovanni e Paolo · S. Giovanni Crisostomo · Palazzo van Axel · Colleoni Monument · Palazzo Pisani · Ospedaletto · Teatro Malibran · Campo S. Marina · Fondaco dei Tedeschi · Rialto 1, 82, N · Palazzo Priuli · S. Lio · Campo di S. Maria Formosa · S. Lorenzo · S. Salvador · S. Maria Formosa · S. Maria della Fava · Palazzo Grimani · Scuola di S. Giorgio degli Schiavoni · Palazzo Querini Stampalia · Palazzo Zorzi · Palazzo Trevisan · S. Giovanni in Oleo · S. Giorgio dei Greci · S. Antonino · S. Marco · C. SS. Filippo e Giacomo · Museo Diocesano · S. Zaccaria · La Pietà · Palazzo Ducale · Riva degli Schiavoni · S. Zaccaria 1, 14, 20, 41, 42, 51, 52, 82, N, LN · Piazza S. Marco · 0 100 m · N

metres long, 38 metres wide at the transepts, 33 metres high in the centre – houses the tombs of some twenty-five other doges.

The finest funerary monuments are in the **chancel**, where Doge Michele Morosini, who ruled for just four months before dying of plague in 1382,

is buried in the tomb at the front on the right, a work which to Ruskin's eyes showed "the exactly intermediate condition of feeling between the pure calmness of early Christianity, and the boastful pomp of the Renaissance faithlessness". Full-blown Renaissance pomp is represented by the tomb of Doge Andrea Vendramin (d.1478), diagonally opposite, while one of the earliest examples of Renaissance style in Venice – Pietro Lombardo's tomb for Doge Pasquale Malipiero (d.1462) – is to be found in the left aisle, to the left of the door to the sacristy. (The sacristy itself contains an excellent painting, Alvise Vivarini's *Christ Carrying the Cross*.) The Lombardo family were also responsible for the tombs of Doge Giovanni Mocenigo and Doge Pietro Mocenigo, to the right and left of the main door. Close by, the second altar of the right aisle is adorned by one of Zanipolo's finest paintings, **Giovanni Bellini**'s polyptych of *SS Vincent Ferrer, Christopher and Sebastian*.

At the top of the right aisle, *St Dominic in Glory*, the only ceiling panel in Venice by Giambattista Piazzetta, Giambattista Tiepolo's tutor, covers the vault of the **Cappella di San Domenico**, alongside which is a tiny shrine containing a relic of St Catherine of Siena. She died in 1380 and her body promptly entered the relic market – most of it is in Rome, but her head is in Siena, one foot is here and other lesser relics are scattered about Italy. Round the corner, in the south transept, two other superb paintings hang close together: a *Coronation of the Virgin* attributed to Cima da Conegliano and Giovanni Martini da Udine, and Lorenzo Lotto's *St Antonine* (1542).

And don't miss the **Cappella del Rosario**, at the end of the north transept. In 1867 a fire destroyed its paintings by Tintoretto, plus Giovanni Bellini's *Madonna* and Titian's *Martyrdom of St Peter*, San

Zanipolo's two most celebrated paintings. A lengthy twentieth-century restoration made use of surviving fragments and installed other pieces such as Veronese's ceiling panels of *The Annunciation*, *The Assumption* and *The Adoration of the Shepherds*, and another *Adoration* by him on the left of the door.

The Colleoni monument

When he died in 1475, the mercenary captain **Bartolomeo Colleoni** left a legacy of some 700,000 ducats to the Venetian state. But there was a snag: the Signoria could have the money only if an **equestrian monument** to him were erected in the square before San Marco – an unthinkable proposition to Venice's rulers, with their cult of anonymity. The problem was circumvented with a fine piece of disingenuousness, by which Colleoni's will was taken to permit the raising of the statue before the Scuola di San Marco, rather than the Basilica. **Andrea Verrocchio**'s statue wasn't finally unveiled until 1496, but the wait was certainly worth it: this idealized image of steely masculinity is one of the masterpieces of Renaissance sculpture.

The Scuola Grande di San Marco

Colleoni's backdrop, the **Scuola Grande di San Marco**, now provides a sumptuous facade and foyer for Venice's hospital. The facade was started by Pietro Lombardo and Giovanni Buora in 1487, half a century after the *scuola* moved here from its original home over in the Santa Croce sestiere, and finished in 1495 by Mauro Codussi. Taken as a whole, the perspectival panels by Tullio and Antonio

Lombardo might not quite create the intended illusion, but they are nonetheless among the most charming sculptural pieces in Venice.

The Ospedaletto

Thurs–Sat: April–Sept 3.30–6.30pm; Oct–March 3–6pm.

Another hospital block is attached to the church of the Ospedaletto (or Santa Maria dei Derelitti), beyond the east end of Zanipolo. The leering giants' heads and over-ripe decorations of its facade made it "the most monstrous" building in the city, according to Ruskin. The much less extravagant interior has a series of eighteenth-century paintings high on the walls above the arches, one of which – *The Sacrifice of Isaac* – is an early Giambattista Tiepolo (fourth on the right). The adjoining music room (€2), frescoed in the eighteenth century, is still used for concerts, many of them free.

Santa Maria Formosa

Mon–Sat 10am–5pm, Sun 1–5pm. €2.50, or Chorus Pass.

The wide **Campo di Santa Maria Formosa**, virtually equidistant from the Piazza, San Zanipolo and the Ponte di Rialto, is a major confluence of routes on the east side of the Canal Grande, and one of the most attractive and atmospheric squares in the city.

The church of Santa Maria Formosa was founded in the seventh century by San Magno, Bishop of Oderzo, who was guided by a dream in which he saw the Madonna *formosa* – a word which most closely translates as buxom and beautiful.

▲ CAMPANILE OF SANTA MARIA FORMOSA

Outside, the most unusual feature is the face at the base of the campanile: it's been argued that it is both a talisman against the evil eye and a piece of clinical realism, portraying a man with a disorder of the sort that disfigured the so-called Elephant Man. The church contains two good paintings. Entering from the west side, the first one you'll see is Bartolomeo Vivarini's triptych of *The Madonna of the Misericordia* (1473), in a nave chapel on the right-hand side of the church. Nearby, closer to the main altar, is Palma il Vecchio's *St Barbara* (1522–24), praised by George Eliot as "an almost unique presentation of a hero-woman". Barbara is the patron saint of artillerymen, which is why the painting shows her treading on a cannon.

Santa Maria della Fava

Daily 8.30am–noon & 4.30–7.30pm.

Between Santa Maria Formosa

and the Rialto stands the church of Santa Maria della Fava (or Santa Maria della Consolazione), whose peculiar name derives from a sweet cake called a *fava* (bean), once an All Souls' Day speciality of a local baker and still a seasonal treat. On the first altar on the right stands Giambattista Tiepolo's early *Education of the Virgin* (1732); on the other side of the church there's *The Madonna and St Philip Neri*, painted five years earlier by Giambattista Piazzetta.

The Querini-Stampalia

Tues–Thurs & Sun 10am–6pm, Fri & Sat 10am–10pm. €8.

On the south side of Campo di Santa Maria Formosa, a footbridge over a narrow canal leads into the **Palazzo Querini-Stampalia**, home of the Pinacoteca Querini-Stampalia. Although there is a batch of Renaissance pieces here, the general tone is set by the culture of eighteenth-century Venice, a period to which much of the palace's decor belongs. The winningly inept pieces by Gabriel Bella form a comprehensive record of Venetian social life in that century, and the more accomplished genre paintings of Pietro and Alessandro Longhi feature prominently as well. Make sure you take a look at the **gardens** and ground-floor exhibition space – they were redesigned in the 1960s by the sleek modernist Carlo Scarpa. On Friday and Saturday the Querini-

Stampalia offers an additional diversion, when concerts by the Scuola di Musica Antica di Venezia (at 5pm and 8.30pm) are included in the price of the entrance ticket.

The Museo Diocesano

Daily 10.30am–12.30pm. Donation requested. Beside the Rio di Palazzo, at the back of the Palazzo Ducale, stands the early fourteenth-century cloister of Sant'Apollonia, the only Romanesque cloister in the city. Fragments from the Basilica di San Marco dating back to the ninth century are displayed here, and a miscellany of sculptural pieces from other churches are on show in the adjoining Museo Diocesano d'Arte Sacra where the permanent collection consists chiefly of a range of religious artefacts and paintings gathered from churches that have closed down or entrusted their possessions to the safety of the museum. In addition, freshly restored works from other collections or churches sometimes pass through here, giving the museum an edge of unpredictability.

San Zaccaria

Daily 10am–noon & 4–6pm.

East of Sant'Apollonia, the

▼ BELLINI'S SAN ZACCARIA ALTARPIECE

▲ RIVA DEGLI SCHIAVONI

Salizzada di San Provolo, leading east out of Campo Santi Filippo e Giacomo, runs straight to the elegant **Campo San Zaccaria**, a spot with a chequered past. In 864 **Doge Pietro Tradonico** was murdered in the campo as he returned from vespers, and in 1172 **Doge Vitale Michiel II**, having not only blundered in peace negotiations with the Byzantine empire but also brought the plague back with him from Constantinople, was murdered as he fled for the sanctuary of San Zaccaria.

Founded in the ninth century as a shrine for the body of Zaccharias, father of John the Baptist, the church of San Zaccaria had already been rebuilt several times when, in 1444, Antonio Gambello embarked on a massive rebuilding project that was concluded some seventy years later by Mauro Codussi, who took over the facade from the first storey upwards. The end result is a distinctively Venetian mixture of Gothic and Renaissance styles.

The interior's notable architectural feature is its **ambulatory**: unique in Venice, it might have been built to accommodate the annual ritual of the doges' Easter Sunday visit. Nearly every inch of wall surface is hung with seventeenth- and eighteenth-century paintings, all of them outshone by Giovanni **Bellini**'s large *Madonna and Four Saints* (1505), on the second altar on the left. The €1 fee payable to enter the Cappella di Sant'Atanasio and Cappella di San Tarasio (off the right aisle) is well worth it for the three wonderful composite altarpieces by Antonio Vivarini and Giovanni d'Alemagna (all 1443). Downstairs is the spooky and perpetually waterlogged ninth-century crypt, the burial place of eight early doges.

The Riva degli Schiavoni

The broad Riva degli Schiavoni, stretching from the edge of the Palazzo Ducale to the canal just before the Arsenale entrance, is constantly thronged during the day, with an unceasing flow of promenading tourists and passengers hurrying to and from its vaporetto stops, threading through the souvenir stalls and past the wares of the African street vendors. The Riva has long been one of Venice's smart addresses. Petrarch and his daughter lived at no. 4145 in 1362–67, and Henry James stayed at no. 4161, battling against constant distractions to finish *The Portrait of a Lady*. George Sand, Charles Dickens, Proust, Wagner and the ever-present Ruskin all checked in at the *Hotel Danieli* (see p.166).

La Pietà

Daily 10am–noon & 4–6pm.

The main eyecatcher on the Riva is the white facade of Santa Maria della Visitazione, known less cumbersomely as La Pietà. **Vivaldi** wrote many of his finest pieces for the orphanage attached to the church, where he worked as violin-master (1704–18) and later as choirmaster (1735–38). During Vivaldi's second term Giorgio Massari won a competition to rebuild the church, and it's probable that the composer advised him on acoustics, though building didn't began until after Vivaldi's death. The white and gold interior is crowned by a superb **ceiling painting** of *The Glory of Paradise* by Giambattista Tiepolo. Unfortunately the Pietà is still one of Venice's busiest music venues, mostly for second-rate renditions of Vivaldi favourites, and custodians of the Pietà box office tend to pull a heavy curtain across the inside door, to stop anyone taking a free look.

The Greek quarter

A couple of minutes' walk north of La Pietà the campanile of **San Giorgio dei Greci** (Mon–Sat 9.30am–1pm & 3.30–5.30pm, Sun 9am–1pm) lurches spectacularly canalwards. The **Greek** presence in Venice was strong from the eleventh century, and became stronger still after the Turkish seizure of Constantinople. Built a century later, the church has Orthodox architectural elements including a *matroneo* (women's gallery) above the main entrance and an iconostasis (or rood screen) that completely cuts off the high altar. The icons on the screen include a few Byzantine pieces dating back as far as the twelfth century.

The Scuola di San Nicolò dei Greci, to the left of the church, now houses the **Museo di Dipinti Sacri Bizantini** (daily 9am–5pm; €4), a collection of predominantly fifteenth- to eighteenth-century icons, many of them by the *Madoneri*, the school of Greek and Cretan artists working in Venice in that period.

▲ FILIPPI EDITORE VENEZIA

Shops

Filippi Editore Venezia

Caselleria 5284 & Calle del Paradiso 5763. Mon–Sat 9am–12.30pm & 3–7.30pm. The family-run Filippi business produces a vast range of Venice-related facsimile editions, including Francesco Sansovino's sixteenth-century guide to the city (the first city guide ever published) and sells an amazing stock of books about Venice in its two shops.

Kerer

Palazzo Trevisan-Cappello, on Rio Canonica. Daily 9.30am–6pm.
Occupying part of a huge palazzo at the rear of the Basilica di San Marco, this vast showroom sells a wide range of lace, both affordable and exclusive.

Cafés, pasticcerie and gelaterie

Didovich

Campo Marina 5910. Open Mon–Sat till 8pm.
A highly regarded *pasticceria* – some say with the city's best tiramisù and *pastine* (aubergine, pumpkin and other savoury tarts). Standing room only inside, but has outdoor tables.

La Boutique del Gelato

Salizzada S. Lio 5727. Open daily. Closed Dec & Jan.
Top-grade ice creams – the very best in Venice, maybe – at this small outlet.

▲ ACIUGHETA

Rosa Salva

Campo SS Giovanni e Paolo. Closed Wed. With its marble-topped bar and outside tables within the shadow of Zanipolo, this is the most characterful of the three Rosa Salva branches. The coffee and home-made ice cream are superb.

Restaurants

Aciugheta

Campo SS Filippo e Giacomo 4357, ☎041.522.4292. Closed Wed.
A bar with a sizeable pizzeria-*trattoria* attached. The closest spot to San Marco to eat without paying through the nose, it draws a lot of its custom from waterbus staff and gondoliers. Good bar food – in fact, it's generally better than you get in the restaurant section. The name translates as "the little anchovy" and there are paintings of anchovies on the wall.

Alle Testiere

Calle Mondo Nuovo 5801
☎041.522.7220. Closed Sun & Mon,
and mid-July to mid-Aug.
Very small mid-range seafood
restaurant near Santa Maria
Formosa, with excellent daily
specials and a superb wine
selection. Sittings at 7pm and
9pm to handle the demand.

Bandierette

Barbaria delle Tole 6671
☎041.522.0619. Closed Mon eve &
Tues. Nice seafood dishes served
by nice people at nice prices
– around €35 a head. It has a
loyal local following, so it's best
to book your table.

Da Remigio

Salizzada dei Greci 3416
☎041.523.0089. Closed Mon eve &
Tues. Brilliant *trattoria*, serving
gorgeous home-made *gnocchi*. Be
sure to book – the locals pack
this place every night. Prices
are rising in tandem with its
burgeoning reputation, but are
still reasonable.

Bars and snacks

Al Portego

Calle Malvasia 6015. Closed Sun.
In the middle of the day this
bar is crammed with customers
eating *cicheti*, and in the evening
there's often a queue for a place
at one of the tiny tables, where
some well-prepared basics (pasta,
risotto, etc) are served. No
reservations are taken, and the
kitchen closes at 9.30pm.

Cip Ciap

Calle Mondo Nuovo 5799. Open 9am–
9pm, closed Tues.
Located across the canal from
the west side of Santa Maria
Formosa, this place offers the
widest range of take-out pizza
slices (*pizza al taglio*) in the city.

Enoteca Mascareta

Calle Lunga S. Maria Formosa 5183.
Mon–Sat 6pm–1am.
Buzzing wine bar with delicious
snacks.

L'Olandese Volante

Campo S. Lio. Open until 12.30am, Fri
& Sat until 2am, closed Sun morning.
The "Flying Dutchman" is a
busy brasserie-style pub with
plenty of outdoor tables.

Osteria da Baco

Calle delle Rasse 4620. Open daily until
midnight or later.
Traditional-style *osteria*, with
a wide selection of filling
sandwiches.

Eastern Castello

For all that most visitors see of the eastern section of the Castello *sestiere*, the city may as well peter out a few metres to the east of San Zanipolo. Sights are thinly spread here, and a huge bite is taken out of the area by the dockyards of the Arsenale, yet the slab of the city immediately to the west of the Arsenale contains places that shouldn't be ignored – the Renaissance San Francesco della Vigna, for example, and the Scuola di San Giorgio degli Schiavoni, with its endearing cycle of paintings by Carpaccio. And although the mainly residential area beyond the Arsenale has little to offer in the way of cultural monuments other than the ex-cathedral of San Pietro di Castello and the church of Sant'Elena, it would be a mistake to leave the easternmost zone unexplored. For one thing, the whole length of the waterfront gives spectacular panoramas of the city, with the best coming last.

San Francesco della Vigna

Daily 8am–12.30pm & 3–6.30pm.
The area that lies to the **east of San Zanipolo** is not an attractive district at first sight, but carry on east for just a couple of minutes and a striking Renaissance facade blocks your way. The ground occupied by San Francesco della Vigna has a hallowed place in the mythology of Venice, as according to tradition it was around here that the angel appeared to Saint Mark to tell him that the lagoon islands were to be his final resting place. Begun in 1534, the present building was much modified in the course of its construction. Palladio was brought in to provide the facade, a feature that looks like something of an afterthought from the side, but which must have been stunning at the time. The **interior** has some fine works of art, notably a glowingly colourful *Madonna and Child Enthroned* by Antonio da Negroponte (right transept), marvellous sculpture

▼ SAN FRANCESCO DELLA VIGNA

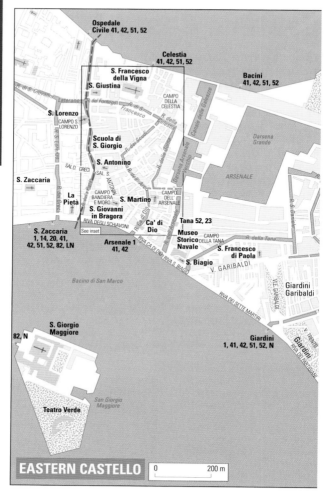

EASTERN CASTELLO

0   200 m

by the Lombardo family in the Giustiniani chapel (left of the chancel) and a *Sacra Conversazione* by Veronese (last chapel of the left aisle). A door at the end of the transept leads to a pair of tranquil fifteenth-century cloisters, via the **Cappella Santa**, which has a *Madonna and Child* by Giovanni Bellini and assistants.

The Scuola di San Giorgio degli Schiavoni

April–Oct Tues–Sat 9.30am–12.30pm & 3.30–6.30pm, Sun 9.30am–12.30pm; Nov–March Tues–Sat 10am–12.30pm & 3–6pm, Sun 10am–12.30pm. €3.

Venice has two brilliant cycles of pictures by **Vittore Carpaccio**, one of the most disarming of Venetian artists – one is in the

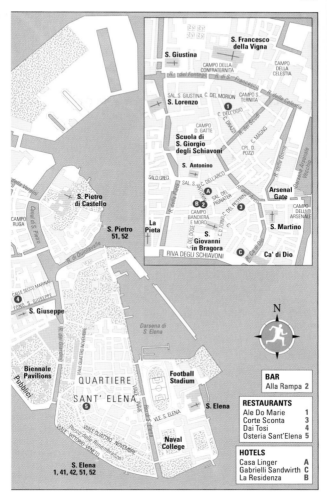

Accademia, the other in the Scuola di San Giorgio degli Schiavoni, the confraternity of Venice's Slavic community. The cycle illustrates mainly the lives of the Dalmatian patron saints – George, Tryphone and Jerome. As always with Carpaccio, what holds your attention is not so much the main event as the incidental details with which he packs the scene, such as the limb-strewn feeding-ground of St George's dragon, or the endearing little white dog in *The Vision of St Augustine* (he was writing to St Jerome when a vision told him of Jerome's death).

San Giovanni in Brágora

Mon–Sat 9–11am & 3.30–5.30pm.

San Giovanni in Brágora is probably best known to Venetians as the baptismal church of Antonio Vivaldi. The church is dedicated to the Baptist, and some people think that its strange suffix is a reference to a region from which some relics of the saint were once brought; others link the name to the old dialect words for mud (*brago*) and backwater (*gora*). The present structure was begun in 1475, and its best paintings were created within a quarter-century of the rebuilding: a triptych by **Bartolomeo Vivarini**, on the wall between the first and second chapels on the right; a *Resurrection* by **Alvise Vivarini**, to the left of the sacristy door; and two paintings by **Cima da Conegliano** – *SS Helen and Constantine*, to the right of the sacristy door, and a *Baptism* on the high altar.

The Arsenale

A corruption of the Arabic *darsin'a* (house of industry), the very name of the Arsenale is indicative of the strength of Venice's links with the eastern Mediterranean, and the workers of these dockyards and factories were the foundations upon which the city's maritime supremacy rested. By the 1420s it had become the base for some three hundred shipping companies, operating around three thousand vessels of two hundred tons or more; at the Arsenale's zenith, around the middle of the sixteenth century, its wet and dry docks, its rope and sail factories, its ordnance depots and gunpowder mills employed a total of 16,000 men – equal to the population of a major town of the period.

There is no public access to the Arsenale, but you can inspect the magnificent **gateway** at close quarters. The first structure in Venice to employ the classical vocabulary of Renaissance architecture, it is guarded by four photogenic lions brought here from Greece: the two furthest on the right probably came from the Lion Terrace at Delos, and date from around the sixth century BC; the larger pair were stolen from Piraeus in 1687 by Francesco Morosini.

The Museo Storico Navale

Mon–Fri 8.45am–1.30pm, Sat 8.45am–1pm. €1.60.

Documenting every conceivable facet of Venice's naval history, the Museo Storico Navale is a somewhat diffuse museum, but a selective tour is an essential supplement to a walk round the Arsenale district. Improbable though it sounds, the models of Venetian craft – from the gondola to the 224-oar fighting galley and the last *Bucintoro* (the state ceremonial

▲ ARSENALE GATE

galley) – will justify the entrance fee for most people.

Via Garibaldi and San Pietro di Castello

In 1808 the greater part of the canal connecting the Bacino di San Marco to the broad northeastern inlet of the Canale di San Pietro was filled in to form what is now Via Garibaldi, the widest street in the city and the social hub of the eastern district. Via Garibaldi points the way to the island of **San Pietro**, one of the first parts of central Venice to be inhabited. Nowadays this is a workaday district where the repairing of boats is the main occupation, yet it was once the ecclesiastical centre of Venice, having been the seat of the **Patriarch of Venice** until 1807. As with the Arsenale, the history of San Pietro is somewhat more interesting than what you can see. The present San Pietro di Castello (Mon–Sat 10am–5pm, Sun 1–5pm; €2.50 or Chorus Pass) is a fairly uncharismatic church, its most interesting features being the stone-clad and precarious **campanile**, and the so-called **Throne of St Peter** (in the right aisle), a marble seat made in the thirteenth century from an Arabic funeral stone cut with texts from the Koran. A late work by Veronese, *SS John the Evangelist, Peter and Paul,* hangs by the entrance to the Cappello Lando (left aisle), where you'll find a bust of St Lorenzo Giustiniani, the first Patriarch of Venice. Giustinani, who died in 1456, lies in the glass case within the elaborate high altar, which was designed by Longhena.

The public gardens and the Biennale site

Stretching from Via Garibaldi

▲ SANT'ELENA

to the Rio di Sant'Elena, the arc of green spaces formed by the **Giardini Garibaldi, Giardini Pubblici** and **Parco delle Rimembranze** provide a remedy for the claustrophobia that overtakes most visitors to Venice at some point. Largely obscured by the trees are the rather more extensive grounds belonging to the Biennale, a dormant zone except when the art and architecture shindigs are in progress (in the summer of odd- and even-numbered years respectively; see p.179). Various countries have built permanent pavilions for their Biennale representatives, forming a unique colony that features work by some of the great names of modern architecture and design, such as Alvar Aalto, Gerrit Thomas Rietveld and Carlo Scarpa.

Sant'Elena

Mon–Sat 5–7pm.

The island of Sant'Elena, the city's eastern limit, was greatly enlarged during the Austrian administration, partly to furnish accommodation and exercise grounds for the occupying troops. Its sole monument is Sant'Elena church, founded in the thirteenth century to house the body of St Helena, Constantine's mother. Approached between the walls of the naval college and the ramshackle home of Venice's second-division football team, it's worth visiting for the fine **doorway**, an ensemble incorporating the **monument to Vittore Cappello**, captain-general of the republic's navy in the 1460s, showing him kneeling before St Helena.

▲ ALE DO MARIE

Restaurants

Ale do Marie

Calle dell'Ogio 3129 ☎ 041.296.0424. Closed Mon. Established a century ago, this is one of the very few simple neighbourhood *trattorie* left in Venice. Honest food, honest prices.

Corte Sconta

Calle del Pestrin 3886 ☎ 041.522.7024. Closed Sun & Mon. Secreted in a lane to the east of San Giovanni in Brágora, on the route to San Martino, this restaurant is a candidate for the title of Venice's finest. The exceptionally pleasant staff tend to make it difficult to resist ordering the day's specials, which could easily result in a bill in the region of €70 each – and it would be just about the best meal you could get in Venice for that price. Booking several days in advance essential for most of the year.

Dai Tosi

Calle Secco Marina 738 ☎ 041.523.7102. Open till 11.30pm, closed Wed. Lively pizzeria-*trattoria* with a devoted clientele – you'd be well advised to book at the weekend. There's a bar in front of the small dining room, where they mix the house aperitif: *sgropino*, a delicious mingling of vodka, lemon and prosecco.

Osteria Sant'Elena

Calle Chinotto 24 ☎ 041.520.8419. Open till midnight, closed Tues. This utterly genuine neighbourhood restaurant is the preserve of the residents of Sant'Elena except when the Biennale is in full swing. The menu is simple, the cooking good, prices fair and there's a bar serving *cicheti* at the front; outside tables add to the appeal.

Bar and snacks

Alla Rampa

Salizzada S. Antonin 3607. Closed Sun. This grittily traditional bar has been run for more than forty years by the no-nonsense Signora Leli. Great for an inexpensive glass, if you don't mind being the only customer who isn't a Venetian male.

The Canal Grande

The Canal Grande is Venice's high street, and divides the city in half, with three *sestieri* to the west and three to the east. Pending the construction of the much-discussed bridge to link the bus and train stations, only three **bridges** cross the waterway – at the station, Rialto and Accademia – but a number of **gondola traghetti** provide additional crossing points at regular intervals, as does the #1 **vaporetto**, which slaloms from one bank to the other along its entire length. The Canal Grande is almost four kilometres long and varies in width between thirty and seventy metres; it is, however, surprisingly shallow, at no point much exceeding five metres.

The section that follows is principally a selection of **Canal Grande palaces** – the churches and other public buildings that you can see from the vaporetto are covered in the appropriate geographical sections. It's arranged as two consecutive sections, with the left bank (ie the left as you travel down from the train station) followed by the right bank; surveying both banks simultaneously is possible only if you happen to get a prime seat right at the front or the back of a vaporetto.

The Left Bank

If you come into Venice by train, your first sight of the Canal Grande will be from the upper stretch of its left bank, with the vaporetto landing stages directly in front. To the right should be the newest of the Canal Grande's bridges, the **Ponte Calatrava**, which is planned to connect to the bus

Venetian palazzi

Virtually all the surviving Canal Grande palaces were built over a span of about five hundred years, and in the course of that period the **basic plan** varied very little. The typical Venetian palace has an entrance hall (the **andron**) on the ground floor, and this runs right through the building, flanked by storage rooms. Above comes the mezzanine floor – the small rooms on this level were used as offices or, from the sixteenth century onwards, as libraries or living rooms. On the next floor – often the most extravagantly decorated – you find the **piano nobile**, the main living area, arranged as suites of rooms on each side of a central hall (**portego**), which runs, like the andron, from front to back. The plan of these houses can be read from the outside of the palace, where you'll usually see a cluster of large windows in the centre of the facade, between symmetrically placed side windows. Frequently there is a second *piano nobile* above the first – this generally would have been accommodation for relatives or children (though sometimes it was the main living quarters). The attic would have been used for servants' rooms or storage.

The Canal Grande

△ Piazzale Roma

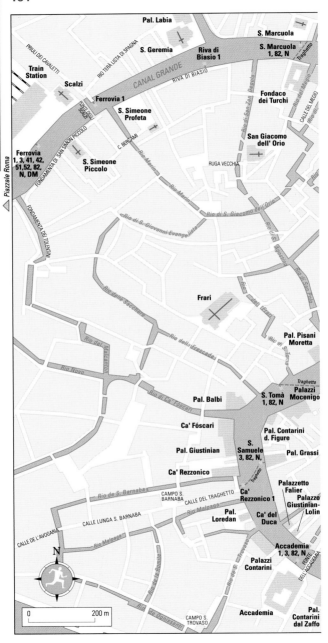

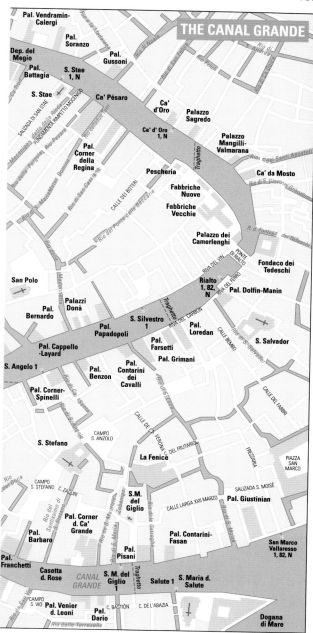

THE CANAL GRANDE

Pal. Vendramin-Calergi
Pal. Soranzo
Dep. del Megio
Pal. Battagia
S. Stae 1, N
Pal. Gussoni
S. Stae
Ca' Pésaro
Ca' d'Oro
Palazzo Sagredo
Ca' d' Oro 1, N
Palazzo Mangilli-Valmarana
Pal. Corner della Regina
Pescheria
Ca' da Mosto
Fabbriche Nuove
Fabbriche Vecchie
Palazzo dei Camerlenghi
PONTE DI RIALTO
Fondaco dei Tedeschi
San Polo
RIVA DEL VIN
Rialto 1, 82, N
RIVA DEL FERRO
Pal. Dolfin-Manin
Palazzi Donà
Pal. Bernardo
S. Silvestro 1
RIVA DEL CARBON
Pal. Loredan
S. Salvador
Pal. Papadopoli
Pal. Farsetti
Pal. Cappello-Layard
Pal. Grimani
S. Angelo 1
Pal. Benzon
Pal. Contarini dei Cavalli
Pal. Corner-Spinelli
CAMPO S. ANZOLO
S. Stefano
La Fenice
PIAZZA SAN MARCO
CAMPO S. STEFANO
SALIZADA S. MOISÉ
Pal. Corner d. Ca' Grande
S.M. del Giglio
Pal. Giustinian
Pal. Barbaro
Pal. Contarini-Fasan
San Marco Vallaresso 1, 82, N
Pal. Franchetti
Casetta d. Rose
S. M. del Giglio 1
Salute 1
S. Maria d. Salute
CANAL GRANDE
Pal. Venier d. Leoni
Pal. Dario
Dogana di Mare
Pal. Pisani

station but has become bogged down in legal arguments. Downstream, more or less in front of the station, lies the **Ponte degli Scalzi**, successor to an iron structure put up by the Austrians in 1858–60; like the one at the Accademia, it was replaced in the early 1930s to give the new steamboats sufficient clearance.

Palazzo Labia

The boat passes two churches, the Scalzi and San Geremia, before the first of the major palaces comes into view – the Palazzo Labia (completed c.1750). The main facade of the building stretches along the Cannaregio canal, but from the Canal Grande you can see how the side wing wraps itself round the campanile of the neighbouring church – such interlocking is common in Venice, where maximum use has to be made of available space. See also p.108.

Palazzo Vendramin-Calergi

Not far beyond the unfinished church of **San Marcuola** stands the Palazzo Vendramin-Calergi. Begun by Mauro Codussi at the very end of the fifteenth

century, this was the first Venetian palace built on classical Renaissance lines. The palazzo's most famous resident was Richard Wagner, who died here in February 1883. It's now the home of Venice's casino.

Ca' d'Oro

The most beguiling palace on the canal is the Ca' d'Oro. (*Ca'* is an abbreviation of *casa di stazio*, meaning the main family home; it was only after the fall of the Republic that the "Casa" was dropped in favour of "Palazzo".) Incorporating fragments of a thirteenth-century palace that once stood on the site, the Ca' d'Oro was built in the 1420s and 30s, and acquired its nickname – "The Golden House" – from the gilding that used to accentuate much of its carving. See also p.113.

Ca' da Mosto

The arches of the first floor of the Ca' da Mosto and the carved panels above them are remnants of a thirteenth-century Veneto-Byzantine building, and are thus among the oldest structures to be seen on the Canal Grande. Alvise da Mosto,

▼ THE RIALTO BRIDGE

discoverer of the Cape Verde Islands, was born here in 1432; by the end of that century the palazzo had become the *Albergo del Lion Bianco*, and from then until the nineteenth century it was one of Venice's most popular hotels.

▲ PALAZZO LOREDAN (CENTRE) AND PALAZZO FARSETTI (RIGHT)

Fondaco dei Tedeschi

The huge building just before the Rialto Bridge is the Fondaco dei Tedeschi, once headquarters of the city's German merchants. The German traders were the most powerful foreign grouping in the city, and as early as 1228 they were leased a building on this central site. In 1505 the Fondaco burned down; Giorgione and Titian were commissioned to paint the exterior of the new fondaco. The remains of their contribution are now in the Ca' d'Oro. The Fondaco has been renovated several times since the sixteenth century, and is now the main post office.

Rialto Bridge

The famous Ponte di Rialto superseded a succession of wooden structures – one of Carpaccio's *Miracles of the True Cross*, in the Accademia, shows you one of them. The decision to construct a stone bridge was taken in 1524, and eventually the job was awarded to the aptly named **Antonio da Ponte**, whose top-heavy design was described by Edward Gibbon as "a fine bridge, spoilt by two rows of houses upon it". Until 1854, when the first

Accademia bridge was built, this was the only point at which the Canal Grande could be crossed on foot.

Palazzo Loredan and the Palazzo Farsetti

The Palazzo Loredan and the Palazzo Farsetti, standing side by side at the end of the Riva del Carbon, are heavily restored Veneto-Byzantine palaces of the thirteenth century. The former was the home of Elena Corner Piscopia, who in 1678 graduated from Padua University, so becoming the first woman ever to hold a university degree. The two buildings are now occupied by the town hall.

Palazzo Grimani

Work began on the immense Palazzo Grimani in 1559, to designs by Sanmicheli, but was not completed until 1575, sixteen years after his death. Ruskin, normally no fan of Renaissance architecture, made an exception for this colossal palace, calling it "simple, delicate, and sublime".

The Mocenigo palazzi

Four houses that once all belonged to the Mocenigo family stand side by side on the **Volta del Canal**, as the Canal Grande's sharpest turn is known: the **Palazzo Mocenigo-Nero**, a late sixteenth-century building; the double **Palazzo Mocenigo**, built in the eighteenth century as an extension to the Nero house; and the **Palazzo Mocenigo Vecchio**, a Gothic palace remodelled in the seventeenth century. Byron and his menagerie – a dog, a fox, a wolf and a monkey – lived in the Mocenigo-Nero palace for a couple of years. Much of his time was taken up with a local baker's wife called Margarita Cogni, whose reaction to being rejected by him was to attack him with a table knife and then hurl herself into the Canal Grande.

Palazzo Grassi

The vast palace round the Volta is the Palazzo Grassi, built in 1748–72 by Massari, who supervised the completion of the Ca' Rezzonico on the opposite bank. Its first owners were accepted into the ranks of the nobility in return for a hefty contribution to the war

effort against the Turks in 1718. Nowadays it's owned by the art collector and businessman François Pinault, and is used as an exhibition venue.

Accademia Bridge

As the larger vaporetti couldn't get under the iron Ponte dell'Accademia built by the Austrians in 1854, it was replaced in 1932 by a wooden one – a temporary measure that became permanent with the addition of a reinforcing steel substructure.

Palazzi Franchetti and Barbaro

The huge palazzo at the foot of the bridge is the Palazzo Franchetti, which was built in the fifteenth century and enlarged at the end of the nineteenth; it is sometimes used as an exhibition space. Its neighbours, on the opposite side of the Rio dell'Orso, are the twinned Palazzi Barbaro; the house on the left is early fifteenth-century, the other late seventeenth-century. Henry James, Monet, Whistler, Browning and John Singer Sargent were among the luminaries who stayed in the older Barbaro house in the late nineteenth century: James finished *The Aspern Papers* here, and used it as a setting for *The Wings of a Dove*.

Palazzo Corner della Ca' Grande

The palace that used to stand on the site of the Palazzo Corner della Ca' Grande was destroyed when a fire lit to dry out a stock of sugar in the attic ran out of control, an incident that illustrates the dual commercial-residential function of many palaces in Renaissance Venice. Sansovino's replacement was built from 1545 onwards.

▼ PALAZZO GRASSI

The rugged stonework of the lower storey – a distinctive aspect of many Roman and Tuscan buildings of the High Renaissance – makes it a prototype for the right bank's Ca' Pésaro and Ca' Rezzonico.

Palazzo Contarini-Fasan

The narrow Palazzo Contarini-Fasan – a mid-fifteenth-century palace with unique wheel tracery on the balconies – is popularly known as "the house of Desdemona", but although the model for Shakespeare's heroine did live in Venice, her association with this house is purely sentimental.

The Right Bank

Arriving in Venice by road, you come in on the right bank of the Canal Grande at Piazzale Roma, opposite the train station. Orientation is initially difficult, with canals heading off in various directions and no immediate landmark; it is not until the vaporetto swings round by the train station that it becomes obvious that this is the city's main waterway.

Fondaco dei Turchi

Having passed the green-domed church of **San Simeone Piccolo**, the end of the elongated campo of **San Simeone Grande** and a procession of nondescript buildings, you come to the Fondaco dei Turchi. A private house from the early thirteenth century until 1621, it was then turned over to the Turkish traders in the city, who stayed here until 1838. Although it has been over-restored, the building's towers and long water-level arcade give a reasonably precise

▲ CA' PÉSARO

picture of what a Veneto-Byzantine palace would have looked like. See also p.97.

Ca' Pésaro

A short distance beyond the church of **San Stae** stands the thickly ornamented Ca' Pésaro, bristling with diamond-shaped spikes and grotesque heads. Three houses had to be demolished to make room for this palace and its construction lasted half a century – work finished in 1703, long after the death of the architect, Baldassare Longhena. See also p.94.

Palazzo Corner della Regina

The next large building is the Palazzo Corner della Regina, built in 1724 on the site of the home of **Caterina Cornaro**, Queen of Cyprus (see p.65), from whom the palace takes its name. The base of the Biennale archives, it was formerly the *Monte di Pietà* (municipal pawnshop).

Rialto market

Beyond, there's nothing especially engrossing until you reach the Rialto markets, which begin with the neo-Gothic fish market, the **Pescheria**, built in 1907; there's been a fish market here since the fourteenth century. The older buildings that follow it, the **Fabbriche Nuove di Rialto** and (set back from the water) the **Fabbriche Vecchie di Rialto**, are by Sansovino (1555) and Scarpagnino (1522) respectively. See also p.92.

Palazzo dei Camerlenghi

The large building at the base of the Rialto bridge is the Palazzo dei Camerlenghi (c.1525), the former chambers of the Venetian exchequer. Debtors could find themselves in the cells of the building's bottom storey – hence the name *Fondamenta delle Prigioni* given to this part of the canalside.

Palazzo Balbi

The cluster of palaces at the Volta constitutes one of the city's architectural glories. The Palazzo Balbi, on the near side of the Rio di Ca' Fóscari, is the youngest of the group, a proto-Baroque design executed in the 1580s to plans by Alessandro Vittoria, whose sculpture is to be found in many Venetian churches. Nicolò Balbi is reputed to have been so keen to see his palace finished that he moored a boat alongside the building site so that he could watch the work progressing – and died of a chill caught by sleeping in it.

Ca' Fóscari

On the opposite bank of the vio stands the Ca' Fóscari (c.1435). The largest private house in Venice at the time of its construction, it was the home of one of the more colourful figures of Venetian history, Doge Francesco Fóscari, whose extraordinarily long term of office (34 years) came to an end with his forced resignation. Venice's university now owns the building, which has been undergoing major restoration for several years.

The Palazzi Giustinian

Adjoining it are the Palazzi Giustinian, a pair of palaces built in the mid-fifteenth century for two brothers who wanted attached but self-contained houses. One of the Palazzi Giustinian was **Wagner**'s home for a while – it was here that he wrote the second act of *Tristan und Isolde*, inspired in part by a nocturnal gondola ride.

Ca' Rezzonico

A little farther on comes Longhena's gargantuan Ca' Rezzonico. It was begun in 1667 as a

▲ CA' FÓSCARI

commission from the Bon family, but they were obliged to sell the still unfinished palace to the Rezzonico, a family of Genoese bankers who were so rich they could afford not just to complete the palazzo but to tack a ballroom onto the back as well. Among its subsequent owners was Pen Browning, whose father Robert died here in 1889. See also p.87.

Palazzo Venier dei Leoni

The Venier family, one of Venice's great dynasties (they produced three doges, including the commander of the Christian fleet at Lépanto), had their main base just beyond the Campo San Vio. In 1759 the Veniers began rebuilding their home, but the Palazzo Venier dei Leoni, which would have been the largest palace on the canal, never progressed further than the first storey – hence its alternative name, **Palazzo Nonfinito**. The stump of the building and the platform on which it is raised (itself an extravagant and novel feature) are occupied by the Guggenheim collection of modern art.

Palazzo Dario

The one domestic building of interest between here and the end of the canal is the miniature Palazzo Dario, compared by Henry James to "a house of

▲ DOGANA DI MARE

cards". The palace was built in the late 1480s, and the multicoloured marbles of the facade are characteristic of the work of the Lombardo family.

Dogana di Mare

The focal point of this last stretch of the canal is Longhena's masterpiece, **Santa Maria della Salute** (see p.82), after which comes the Dogana di Mare (Customs House), the Canal Grande's full stop. The figure which swivels in the wind on top of the Dogana's gold ball is said by most to represent Fortune, though others identify it as Justice.

The northern islands

A trip out to the main islands lying to the north of Venice – San Michele, Murano, Burano and Torcello – will reveal the origins of the glass and lace work touted in so many of the city's shops, and give you a glimpse of the origins of Venice itself, embodied in Torcello's magnificent cathedral of Santa Maria dell'Assunta.

To get to the northern islands, the main vaporetto stop is Fondamente Nove (or Nuove), as most of the island services start here or call here. (You can hop on elsewhere in the city, of course – but make sure that the boat is going towards the islands, not away from them.) For San Michele and Murano only, the circular #41 and #42 vaporetti both run every twenty minutes from Fondamente Nove, circling Murano before heading back towards Venice; the #41 follows an anticlockwise route around the city, the #42 a clockwise route. Murano can also be reached by the #DM ("Diretto Murano"), which from around 8am to 6pm runs to the island from Tronchetto via Piazzale Roma and Ferrovia. For Murano, Burano and Torcello the #LN (Laguna Nord) leaves every half-hour from Fondamente Nove for most of the day (hourly early in the morning and evenings), calling first at Murano-Faro before heading on to Mazzorbo and Burano, from where it proceeds, via Treporti, to Punta Sabbioni and the Lido. A shuttle boat runs every half-hour between Burano and Torcello.

San Michele

The high brick wall around the island of San Michele gives way by the landing stage to the elegant white facade of **San Michele in Isola** (daily 7.30am–12.15pm & 3–4pm), designed by Mauro Codussi in 1469. With this building Codussi quietly revolutionized the architecture of Venice, advancing the principles of Renaissance design in the city and introducing the use of Istrian stone as a material for facades. Easy to carve yet resistant to water, Istrian stone had long been used for damp courses, but never before had anyone clad the entire front of a building in it.

▼ SAN MICHELE CEMETERY

▲ SANTI MARIA E DONATO, MURANO

The main part of the island, through the cloisters, is covered by the **cemetery** of Venice (daily: summer 7.30am–6pm; winter 7.30am–4pm), established here by a Napoleonic decree which forbade further burials in the centre of the city. Space is at a premium, and most of the Catholic dead of Venice lie here in cramped conditions for just ten years or so, when their bones are dug up and removed to an ossuary, and the vacated plot is recycled. The city's Protestants, being less numerous, are permitted to stay in their sector indefinitely. In this Protestant section (no. XV) **Ezra Pound**'s grave is marked by a simple slab with his name on it. Adjoining is the Greek and Russian Orthodox area (no. XIV), including the gravestones of **Igor and Vera Stravinsky** and the more elaborate tomb for **Serge Diaghilev**.

Even with its grave-rotation system in operation, the island is reaching full capacity, so it is now being extended, to a design by David Chipperfield, which will place a sequence of formal courtyards lined with wall tombs on the presently unkempt parts of the island, alongside a new funerary chapel and crematorium. It promises to be a beautiful place – and there's a certain appropriateness to the fact that the twenty-first century's first large-scale addition to the Venetian cityscape will be a cross between a necropolis and a philosopher's retreat.

Murano

Murano nowadays owes its fame entirely to its **glass-blowing industry**, and its main fondamente are crowded with shops selling the fruit of the furnaces, some of it fine, most of it repulsive and some of it laughably pretentious.

From the Colonna vaporetto stop (the first after San Michele) you step onto the Fondamenta dei Vetrai, traditionally the core of the glass industry (as the name suggests) and now the principal tourist trap. Towards the far end is the Dominican church of **San Pietro Martire** (daily 9am–noon & 3–6pm), one of only two churches still in service on the island (compared with seventeen when the Republic fell in 1797). Begun

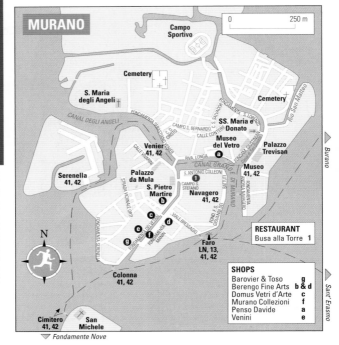

The northern islands

in 1363 but largely rebuilt after a fire in 1474, its main interest lies with its pair of paintings by **Giovanni Bellini** hanging on the right wall.

Murano's one museum is, as you'd expect, devoted to glass. Occupying the seventeenth-century Palazzo Giustinian (formerly home of the bishop of Torcello), the **Museo del Vetro** (April–Oct 10am–5pm; Nov–March 10am–4pm; closed Wed; €4, or Museum Pass/Venice Card) features pieces dating back to the first century and examples of Murano glass from the fifteenth century onwards. Perhaps the finest single item is the dark blue Barovier marriage cup, dating from around 1470; it's on show in room 1 on the first floor, along with some

splendid Renaissance enamelled and painted glass. A separate display, with some captions in English, covers the history of Murano glass techniques – look out for the extraordinary *Murine in Canna*, the method of placing different coloured rods together to form an image in cross-section.

The other Murano church, and the main reason for visiting the island today, is **Santi Maria e Donato** (daily 8am–noon & 4–7pm). It was founded in the seventh century but rebuilt in the twelfth, and is one of the lagoon's best examples of Veneto-Byzantine architecture – the ornate rear apse being particularly fine. The glories of the **interior** are its mosaic floor (dated 1141 in the nave) and the

Venetian glass

Because of the risk of fire, Venice's glass furnaces were moved to Murano from central Venice in 1291, and thenceforth all possible steps were taken to keep the secrets of the trade locked up on the island. Although Muranese workers had by the seventeenth century gained some freedom of movement, for centuries prior to that any glass-maker who left Murano was proclaimed a traitor, and a few were even hunted down. A fifteenth-century visitor judged that "in the whole world there are no such craftsmen of glass as here", and the Muranese were masters of every aspect of their craft. They were producing spectacles by the start of the fourteenth century, monopolized the European manufacture of mirrors for a long time and in the early seventeenth century became so proficient at making coloured crystal that a decree was issued forbidding the manufacture of false gems out of glass, as many were being passed off as authentic stones. The traditional style of Murano glass, typified by the multicoloured floral chandeliers sold in showrooms on Murano and round the Piazza, is still very much in demand. However, in recent years there's been turmoil in the glass industry, due to an inundation of cheap Murano-style tableware and ornaments from Asia and Eastern Europe. Few of Murano's 250 glass companies remain in Venetian hands – the long-established firm of Salviati is French-owned, and even Venini has been bought out, by the Royal Copenhagen company.

arresting twelfth-century mosaic of the Madonna in the apse.

Burano

After the peeling plaster and eroded stonework of the other lagoon settlements, the small, brightly painted houses of Burano come as something of a surprise. Local tradition says that the colours once enabled each fisherman to identify his house from out at sea, but now the colours are used simply for pleasant effect. While many of the men of Burano still depend on the lagoon for their livelihoods, the women's lives are given over to the production and sale of **lace**, and the shops lining the narrow street leading into the village from the vaporetto stop are full of the stuff. Making Burano-point and Venetian-point lace is extremely exacting work, both highly skilled and mind-bendingly repetitive, taking an enormous toll on the eyesight. Each woman specializes in one particular stitch, and as there are seven stitches in all, each piece is passed from woman to woman during its construction. An average-size table centre requires about a month of work.

▲ THE LACE MUSEUM

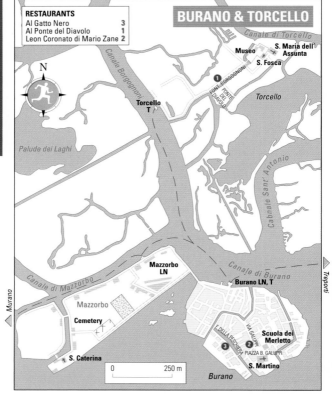

RESTAURANTS
Al Gatto Nero 3
Al Ponte del Diavolo 1
Leon Coronato di Mario Zane 2

BURANO & TORCELLO

Lacemaking is still taught at Burano's **Scuola del Merletto** (April–Oct 10am–5pm; Nov–March 10am–4pm; closed Tues; €4, or Museum/Venice Card), on Piazza Baldassare Galuppi. This *scuola* is simply a school rather than a confraternity-cum-guild (unlike all other craftspeople in Venice, the lacemakers had no guild to represent them, perhaps because the workforce was exclusively female) and it was opened in 1872, when the indigenous crafting of lace had declined so far that it was left to one woman, Francesca Memo, to transmit the necessary skills to a younger generation. Pieces produced here are displayed in the attached **museum**, along with specimens dating back to the sixteenth century; after even a quick tour you'll have no problems distinguishing the real thing from the machine-made and imported lace that fills the Burano shops.

Opposite the lace school stands the church of **San Martino** (daily 8am–noon & 3–7pm), with its drunken campanile; inside, on the second altar on the left, you'll find a fine *Crucifixion* by Giambattista Tiepolo.

Torcello

Torcello has now come full circle. Settled by the very first refugees from the mainland in the fifth century, it became the seat of the bishop of Altinum in 638 and in the following year its cathedral – the oldest building in the lagoon – was founded. By the fourteenth century its population had peaked at around twenty thousand, but Torcello's canals were now silting up, malaria was rife and the ascendancy of Venice was imminent. By the end of the fifteenth century Torcello was largely deserted and today only about thirty people remain in residence.

A Veneto-Byzantine building dating substantially from 1008, the **Cattedrale di Santa Maria dell'Assunta** (daily: March–Oct 10.30am–6pm; Nov–Feb 10am–5pm;€3; joint ticket with campanile or museum €5.50, or €8 with museum and campanile) has evolved from a church founded in the seventh century, of which the crypt and the circular foundations in front of the facade have survived. The dominant tones of the **interior** come from pink brick, gold-based mosaics and the watery green-grey marble of its columns and panelling, which together cast a cool light on the richly patterned eleventh-century mosaic floor. In the apse a stunning twelfth-century mosaic of the Madonna and Child looks down from above a frieze of the Apostles, dating from the middle of the previous century. Below the window, at the Madonna's feet, is a much restored image of St Heliodorus, the first bishop of Altinum. It makes an interesting comparison with the gold-plated face mask on his sarcophagus in front of the high altar, another seventh-century vestige. Mosaic work from the ninth and eleventh centuries adorns the chapel to the right of the high altar, while the other end of the cathedral is dominated by the tumultuous mosaic of the Apotheosis of Christ and the Last Judgement – created in the twelfth century, but renovated in the nineteenth.

Ruskin described the view from the **campanile** (daily: March–Oct 10.30am–5.30pm; Nov–Feb 10am–5pm; €3) as "one of the most notable scenes in this wide world", a verdict you can test for yourself, as the campanile has now been reinforced, cleaned and reopened, after thirty years'

▼ SANTA FOSCA

service as a pigeon-coop.

Torcello's other church, **Santa Fosca** (same hours as cathedral; free), was built in the eleventh and twelfth centuries for the body of the martyred St Fosca, brought to Torcello from Libya some time before 1011 and now resting under the altar. The bare interior exudes a calmness which no number of visitors can quite destroy.

In the square outside sits the curious **chair of Attila**, perhaps once the throne of Torcello's judges in its earliest days. Behind it, the well laid-out **Museo di Torcello** (Tues–Sun: March–Oct 10.30am–5pm; Nov–Feb 10am–4.30pm; €3) includes thirteenth-century gold figures, jewellery, mosaic fragments and a mish-mash of pieces relating to the history of the area.

Shops: Murano glass

Barovier & Toso
Fondamenta dei Vetrai 28 ⓦwww
.barovier.com. Mon–Fri 10am–5pm.

This is a family-run firm which can trace its roots back to the fourteenth century. Predominantly traditional designs.

Berengo Fine Arts
Fondamenta dei Vetrai 109a & Fondamenta Manin 68 ⓦwww
.berengo.com. Daily 10am–6pm.
Berengo has pioneered a new approach to Venetian glass manufacture, with foreign artists' designs being vitrified by Murano glass-blowers.

Domus Vetri d'Arte
Fondamenta dei Vetrai 82. Daily 9.15am–1pm & 2–6pm.
Stocks work by the major postwar Venetian glass designers, artists such as Barbini, Ercole Moretti and Carlo Moretti.

Murano Collezioni
Fondamenta Manin 1c. Daily 10am–6pm. Outlet for work from the Venini, Moretti and Barovier & Toso factories.

Penso Davide
Fondamenta Longa 48. Daily 10am–6pm. The jewellery sold here is both manufactured and designed by the firm, which specializes in giving a new slant to traditional Murano styles. You can watch glass pieces being made in the shop.

Venini
Fondamenta Vetrai 47, ⓦwww.venini.com. Mon–Sat 9.30am–5.30pm.
One of the more adventurous producers, *Venini* often employs designers from other fields of the applied arts.

▲ MURANO GLASS

Shops: Burano lace

Scuola del Merletto
Piazza Baldassare Galuppi.
The lace here is expensive,
but not to a degree that's
disproportionate to the hours
and labour that go into making
it. Be warned that most of the
far cheaper stuff that's sold
from Burano's open-air stalls is
machine-made outside Italy. The
Scuola's lace, on the other hand,
is the finest handmade material.

Restaurants

Al Gatto Nero
Fondamenta Giudecca 88, Burano
℡041.730.120. Closed Mon.
A fine local *trattoria*, just a few
minutes' walk from the busy
Via Galuppi, opposite the
Pescheria. Max, the owner, is a
keen fisherman, and what he
doesn't know about the marine
delicacies of Venice isn't worth
knowing.

Al Ponte del Diavolo
Fondamenta Borgognoni 10/11, Torcello
℡041.730.401. Lunch daily except
Wed, booking essential at weekends.
Open evenings for group bookings only.
The pleasantest restaurant on
Torcello, just before the bridge
it takes its name from, on the

▲ AL GATTO NERO

canal leading from the boat to
the cathedral. Delightful shaded
terrace overlooking the garden.
Prices are moderate, unlike
at the much-hyped *Locanda
Cipriani* near the cathedral.

Busa alla Torre
Campo S. Stefano 3, Murano
℡041.739.662. Closed Mon.
By general agreement, this
moderately priced *trattoria* is by
far the finest fish restaurant on
Murano.

Leon Coronato di Mario Zane
Piazza Baldassare Galuppi 314, Burano
℡041.730.230. Closed Tues.
This homely, friendly and
dependable place serves the best
pizzas on Burano.

The southern islands

The section of the lagoon to the south of the city, enclosed by the long islands of the Lido and Pellestrina, has fewer outcrops of solid land than its northern counterpart. The nearer islands are the more interesting: the Palladian churches of San Giorgio and La Giudecca (linked by the #82 vaporetto) are among Venice's most significant Renaissance monuments, while the alleyways of La Giudecca are full of reminders of the city's manufacturing past. The Venetian tourist industry began with the development of the Lido, which has now been eclipsed by the city itself as a holiday destination, yet still draws thousands of people to its beaches each year. A visit to the Armenian island, San Lazzaro degli Armeni, makes an absorbing afternoon's round trip, and if you have a bit more time to spare you could undertake an expedition to the fishing town of Chioggia, at the southern extremity of the lagoon. The farther-flung settlements along the route to Chioggia may have seen more glorious days, but the voyage out there from the city is a pleasure in itself.

San Giorgio Maggiore

Daily: May–Sept 9.30am–12.30pm & 2–5.30pm; Oct–April 9.30am–12.30pm & 2.30–5pm.

Palladio's church of San Giorgio Maggiore, facing the Palazzo Ducale across the Bacino di San Marco, is one of the most prominent and familiar of all Venetian landmarks. It is a startling building, both on the outside and inside, where white stucco is used to dazzling effect – "Of all the colours,

▲ SAN GIORGIO MAGGIORE

none is more proper for churches than white; since the purity of colour, as of the life, is particularly gratifying to God," wrote Palladio. Two outstanding pictures by **Tintoretto** hang in the chancel: *The Last Supper*, perhaps the most famous of all his works, and *The Fall of Manna*. They were painted as a pair in 1592–94 – the last two years of the artist's life, and a *Deposition* of the same date is in the Cappella dei Morti (through the door on the right of the choir). The door on the left of the choir leads to the **campanile** (€3), the best vantage point in all of Venice.

The adjoining monastery – now occupied by the **Fondazione Giorgio Cini**, which runs various arts research institutes, a naval college and a craft school here – is one of the architectural wonders of the city, featuring two beautiful cloisters and a magnificent refectory by Palladio. Exhibitions are regularly held at the Fondazione; at other times the gatekeeper might allow you a quick look around.

La Giudecca

In the earliest records of Venice the chain of islets now called La Giudecca was known as Spina Longa, a name clearly derived from its shape. The modern name might refer to the Jews (*Giudei*) who lived here from the late thirteenth century until their removal to the Ghetto, but is most likely to originate with the two disruptive noble families who in the ninth century were shoved into this district to keep

▲ VIEW ACROSS GIUDECCA CANAL TO IL REDENTORE

them out of mischief (*giudicati* means "judged"). Giudecca grew into the city's **industrial** inner suburb: Venice's public transport boats used to be made here; an asphalt factory and a distillery were once neighbours at the western end; and the matting industry, originating in the nineteenth century, kept going here until 1950. However, the semi-dereliction of the present-day island is a potent emblem of Venice's loss of economic self-sufficiency. Swathes of La Giudecca are now purely residential areas, but in this respect things are looking up, with a spate of housing developments and ancillary social facilities being funded in recent years. In no other part of Venice are you as likely to see a site occupied by cranes and bulldozers.

The first vaporetto stop after San Giorgio Maggiore is close to the tiny church of the **Zitelle** (open for Mass only, Sun 10am–noon), which

Sacca Fisola
41, 42, 82, N

Gesuati

Zattere
51, 52, 82, N

Mulino
Stucky

Palanca
41, 42, 82, N

Sant'
Eufemia

S.
Cosma

LA GIUDECCA & SAN GIORGIO MAGGIORE

The southern islands PLACES

was built in 1582–86 from plans worked out some years earlier by Palladio, albeit for a different site. La Giudecca's main monument, beyond the tug-boats' mooring and the youth hostel (once a granary; see p.169), is the Franciscan church of **Il Redentore** (Mon–Sat 10am–5pm, Sun 1–5pm; €2.50, or Chorus Pass), designed by **Palladio** in 1577. In 1575–76 Venice suffered an outbreak of plague which killed nearly fifty thousand people – virtually a third of the city's population. The Redentore was built by the Senate in thanks for Venice's deliverance, and

every year until the downfall of the Republic the doge and his senators attended a Mass here to renew their declaration of gratitude, walking to the church over a pontoon bridge from the Zàttere. This is the most sophisticated of Palladio's church projects, but an appreciation of its subtleties is difficult, as a rope prevents visitors going beyond the nave. The best paintings in the church are in the sacristy, which is rarely opened.

At the far end of the island looms the colossal **Mulino Stucky**. With the development of the industrial sector at

▼ VIEW OF PONTE LUNGO, LA GIUDECCA

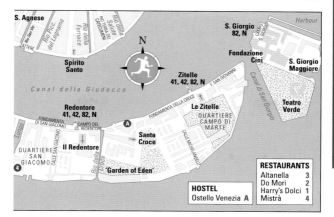

S. Agnese

Rio Pocc
Fornace

Rio della
Fornace

Rio delle
TERRA DEI
CATECUMENI

N

S. Giorgio
82, N

Harbour

S. Giorgio
Maggiore

Spirito
Santo

Fondazione
Cini

Canal della Giudecca

Zitelle
41, 42, 82, N

FONDAMENTA DELLA CROCE

F. SAN GIOVANNI

Canal di San Giorgio

Teatro
Verde

Redentore
41, 42, 82, N

FONDAMENTA
DI SAN GIACOMO

CAMPO DEL
SS. REDENTORE

Le Zitelle

QUARTIERE
CAMPO DI
MARTE

CALLE MICHELANGELO

Il Redentore

Santa
Croce

QUARTIERE
SAN
GIACOMO

CALLE SAN GIACOMO

Rio della
Croce

'Garden of Eden'

HOSTEL
Ostello Venezia A

RESTAURANTS
Altanella	3
Do Mori	2
Harry's Dolci	1
Mistrà	4

Marghera (on the mainland) after World War I, the Stucky flour mill went into a nose dive, and in 1954 it closed. It is now being restored for use as a convention centre and a *Hilton* hotel.

The Lido

The Lido was an unspoilt strip of land until the latter part of the nineteenth century. Byron used to gallop his horses across its fields every day, and as late as 1869 Henry James

Flooding and the barrier

Called the **acqua alta** (high water), the winter flooding of Venice is caused by a combination of seasonal tides, fluctuations in atmospheric pressure in the Adriatic and persistent southeasterly winds, and has always been a feature of Venetian life. In recent years, though, it has been getting worse: between 1931 and 1945 there were just eight serious *aque alte*; in the last decade of the twentieth century there were 44 – most spectacularly on November 4, 1966, when for 48 hours the sea level remained an average of almost two metres above mean high tide. By 2002 the number of annual floods had risen to 110 – not all of them were major, but the statistic is nonetheless indicative of a relentlessly rising trend.

The prospect of global warming and rising sea levels has led to a widespread acceptance of the idea of installing a tidal barrier across the three entrances to the lagoon. Nicknamed **Moisè** (Moses) after the Old Testament's great divider of the waters, this barrier is planned to comprise 79 300-tonne steel flaps, which will lie on the floor of the lagoon, forming a submerged barrage some two kilometres long in total; when the water rises to dangerous level, air will be pumped into the flaps and the barrier will then float upright. In April 2003, more than twenty years after the first plan for Moisè was submitted to the government, Silvio Berlusconi attended a ceremony in Venice to mark the start of work, which is planned for completion in 2011. In the meantime, a host of less extravagant flood-prevention projects have been making progress, with embankments and pavements being rebuilt and raised at numerous flood-prone points, and the 60km of the lagoon's outer coastline being reinforced with stone groynes and artificial reefs to dissipate the energy of the waves.

could describe the island as "a very natural place". Before the century was out, however, it had become the smartest **bathing resort** in Italy, and although it is no longer as chic as it was, there is less room on its beaches now than ever before. Unless you're staying at one of the flashy hotels that stand shoulder to shoulder along the seafront, or are prepared to rent one of their beach huts for the day, you'll have to content yourself with the less groomed **public beaches** at the northern and southern ends of the island. The northern beach is twenty minutes' walk from the vaporetto stop at Piazzale Santa Maria Elisabetta; the southern one, right by the municipal golf course, necessitates a bus journey from the Piazzale, and is consequently less of a crush.

The green-domed Santa Maria della Vittoria might be the most conspicuous Lido monument on the lagoon side of the island (unless you count the huge Campari sign) but at close quarters it is revealed as a thoroughly abject thing. In the vicinity of the Piazzale only the **Fortezza di Sant'Andrea** is of much interest, and you have to admire it from a distance across the water – you get a good view from the church and Franciscan monastery of **San Nicolò**. A stroll along the nearby Via Cipro (facing the San Nicolò vaporetto stop) will bring you to the entrance to Venice's **Jewish cemetery** (guided tours in English every month except Oct; Sun 2.30pm; €8.50; reservations at Museo Ebraico or phone ☎041.715.359), which was founded in 1386 and in places has fallen into eloquent decay.

From the Lido to Chioggia

The trip across the lagoon to Chioggia is a more protracted

The Sposalizio

Every year, for about eight centuries, the Lido was the venue for Venice's Marriage to the Sea, or *Sposalizio*. This ritual, the most operatic of Venice's state ceremonials, began as a way of commemorating the exploits of Doge Pietro Orseolo II, who on Ascension Day of the year 1000 set sail to subjugate the pirates of the Dalmatian coast. (Orseolo's standard, by the way, featured possibly the first representation of what was to become the emblem of Venice – the lion of Saint Mark with its paw on an open book.)

According to legend, the ritual reached its definitive form after the Venetians had brought about the reconciliation of Pope Alexander III and Frederick Barbarossa in 1177; the grateful Alexander is supposed to have given the doge the first of the gold rings with which Venice was married to the Adriatic. It's more likely that the essential components of the ritual – the voyage out to the Porto di Lido in the Bucintoro with an escort of garlanded vessels, the dropping of the ring into the brine "In sign of our true and perpetual dominion" and the disembarkation for a solemn Mass at the church of San Nicolò al Lido – were all fixed by the middle of the twelfth century. In case you're thinking of launching a salvage operation for all those gold rings, a fifteenth-century traveller recorded: "After the ceremony, many strip and dive to the bottom to seek the ring. He who finds it keeps it for his own, and, what's more, lives for that year free from all the burdens to which dwellers in that republic are subject."

▲ LIDO LANDING STAGE

business than simply taking the land bus from Piazzale Roma, but it will give you a curative dose of salt air and an understanding of the lagoon. From Gran Viale Santa Maria Elisabetta – the main street from the Lido landing stage to the sea front – the more or less hourly **#11 bus** goes down to **Alberoni**, where it drives onto a ferry for the five-minute hop to Pellestrina; the 10km to the southern tip of Pellestrina are covered by road, and then you switch from the bus to a steamer for the 25-minute crossing to Chioggia. The entire journey takes about eighty minutes, but be sure to check the timetable carefully at Gran Viale Santa Maria Elisabetta, as not every #11 bus goes all the way to Chioggia. The quickest way **back to Venice** is by bus from the Duomo or Sottomarina to Piazzale Roma, but it's only about twenty minutes quicker than the island-hop route, and ACTV passes are not valid, as this is an extra-urban bus service.

The fishing village of **Malamocco**, about 5km into the expedition, is the successor of the ancient settlement called Metamauco, which in the eighth century was the capital of the lagoon confederation. In 1107 the old town was destroyed by a tidal wave; rebuilt Malamocco's most appealing building – the church's scaled-down replica of the campanile of San Marco – can be seen without getting off the bus.

Fishing and the production of fine pillow-lace are the mainstays of life in the village of **Pellestrina**, which is strung out along nearly a third of the ten kilometres of the next island. There's one remarkable structure here, but you get the best view of it as the boat crosses to Chioggia. This is the **Murazzi**, the colossal walls of Istrian boulders, 4km long and 14m thick at the base, which were constructed at the sides of the Porto di Chioggia to protect Venice from the battering of the sea.

Chioggia is the second largest settlement in the lagoon after Venice, and one of Italy's busiest fishing ports. The boat sets you down at the **Piazzetta Vigo**, at the head of the **Corso**

del Popolo, the principal street in Chioggia's gridiron layout, which runs down to the cathedral, passing close to the **fish market**, the best in the whole lagoon. Inside the **cathedral**, the chapel to the left of the chancel contains half a dozen good eighteenth-century paintings, including one attributed to Tiepolo; they're all but invisible, a drawback that you might regard as a blessing in view of the subjects depicted – *The Torture of Boiling Oil*, *The Torture of the Razors*, *The Beheading of Two Martyrs* and so on. Buses run from the cathedral to **Sottomarina**, Chioggia's downmarket answer to Venice's Lido.

San Lazzaro degli Armeni

Visitors received daily from 3.25pm to 5.25pm; €6; the connecting #20 motoscafo leaves San Zaccaria at 3.10pm and returns within ten minutes of the end of the tour.

No foreign community has a longer pedigree in Venice than the Armenians, whose presence is most conspicuously signalled by the island of San Lazzaro degli Armeni, identifiable from the city by the onion-shaped summit of its campanile. Tours are conducted by one of the priests who currently live in the island's **monastery**, and

you can expect him to be trilingual, at the very least. Reflecting the encyclopedic interests of its occupants, the monastery is in places like a whimsically arranged museum: at one end of the old **library**, for example, a mummified Egyptian body is laid out near the sarcophagus in which it was found, while at the other is a teak and ivory throne that once seated the governor of Delhi. The monastery's collection of precious manuscripts and books – the former going back to the fifth century – is another highlight of the visit, occupying a modern rotunda in the heart of the complex. Elsewhere you'll see antique metalwork, extraordinarily intricate Chinese ivory carvings, a gallery of paintings by Armenian artists, a ceiling panel by the young Giambattista Tiepolo and Canova's figure of Napoleon's infant son, which sits in the chamber where Byron studied while lending a hand with the preparation of an Armenian–English dictionary. If you're looking for an unusual present, you could buy something at the monastery's shop: the old maps and prints of Venice are a bargain.

Restaurants

Altanella

Calle delle Erbe 270, Giudecca ☏ 041.522.7780. Closed Mon & Tues.
Run by the same family for three generations, this mid-range restaurant is highly recommended for its fish dishes and the terrace overlooking the island's central canal. No credit cards.

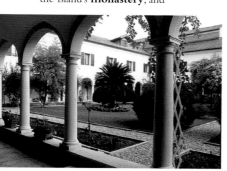

▲ SAN LAZZARO DEGLI ARMENI

Do Mori

Fondamenta Sant'Eufemia 588, Giudecca ℡041.522.5452. Closed Sun. Serves humble pizzas (in the evening) as well as classier fare, with the emphasis, as ever, on fish. For a meal with a view, it can't be bettered.

Harry's Dolci

Fondamenta S. Biagio 773, Giudecca ℡041.522.4844. Open April–Oct; closed Tues. Despite the name, sweets aren't the only things on offer here – the kitchen of this offshoot of *Harry's Bar* is rated by many as the equal of its ancestor. It is appreciably less expensive than *Harry's Bar* (even though many of the dishes are identical), but nonetheless you will be spending in the region of €70 a head, drink excluded. Still, if you want to experience Venetian culinary refinement at its most exquisite, this is it.

Mistrà

Giudecca 212a ℡041.522 0743. Closed Mon eve & Tues.

▲ DO MORI

Occupying the upper storey of a former factory right in the thick of the Giudecca boatyards, *Mistrà* caters mostly for local dockyard workers at lunchtime, when the menu is very brief, very plain and very cheap. In the evenings you'll find a somewhat more refined offering of Venetian fish and seafood, at prices that are higher than the midday dishes, but still extremely reasonable.

Accommodation

Hotels

Venice has well in excess of two hundred **hotels**, ranging from spartan one-star joints to five-star establishments charging way over €1000 per night for the best room in high season; what follows is a rundown of the best choices in all categories. At the end of each review we've indicated the minimum and maximum price for a **double room**; as the minimum price is very rarely on offer, you should expect to pay something far closer to the maximum.

Though there are some typical anomalies, the star system is a broadly reliable indicator of quality, but always bear in mind that you pay through the nose for your proximity to the Piazza. So if you want maximum comfort for your money, decide how much you can afford, then look for a place outside the San Marco *sestiere* – after all, it's not far to walk, wherever you're staying. **Breakfast** is nearly always included in the hotel room rate; if it isn't, you're best advised to take breakfast in a café, where the quality will probably be better and the price certainly lower.

In 2000 Italy's laws relating to tourist accommodation were relaxed, which resulted in the opening of several guest-houses called **locande**, and the appearance of a number of private houses offering bed and breakfast (see p.166). The prefix *locanda* doesn't necessarily indicate an inexpensive place: some upmarket hotels use the label to give their image a more

Booking your accommodation

High season in Venice covers most of the year – officially it runs from March 15 to November 15 and then from December 21 to January 6, but many places don't recognize the existence of a low season any more. (A few hotels, on the other hand, lower their prices in August, a month in which trade can take a bit of a dip, as every Italian knows that Venice can be hellishly hot and clogged with day-trippers during that month.) If you intend to stay in the city at any time during the above periods (or Carnevale), it's wise to book your place at least three months in advance, and for June, July and August it's virtually obligatory to reserve half a year ahead.

If your first-choice hotel is fully booked, your next best option is an internet search – it's not unknown for online agencies such as ⓦ www.web-venice -hotels.com, ⓦ www.venicehotel.com, ⓦ www.bookings.org or ⓦ www.tobook .com to have rooms available in hotels that are nominally full, and even to offer a discount on the hotel's quoted rate. In addition to these, the tourist office's website (ⓦ www.turismovenezia.it) gives details of accommodation of all types, while the Venetian Hoteliers' Association (AVA) lists hundreds of hotels at ⓦ www.veniceinfo .it and ⓦ www.veneziasi.it. Finally, should you bowl into town with nowhere to stay, you could call in at one of the AVA **booking offices**: at the **train station** (daily: summer 8am–9pm; winter 8am–7pm); on the **Tronchetto** (9am–8pm); in the multistorey car park at **Piazzale Roma** (9am–9pm); and at **Marco Polo airport** (summer 9am–7pm; winter noon–7pm). They only deal with hotels (not hostels or B&Bs) and take a deposit that's deductible from your first night's bill.

homely finish. The majority of *locande*, however, are small family-run establishments, offering a standard of accommodation equivalent to three- or even four-star hotels (24-hour room service is just about the only facility they don't provide), but often at considerably lower cost.

San Marco: North of the Piazza

These hotels are marked on the map on pp.64–65

Ai Do Mori Calle Larga S. Marzo 658 ☎041.520.4817, ⓦ www.hotelaidomori .com. Very friendly, and situated a few paces off the Piazza, this is a top recommendation for budget travellers. The top-floor room has a private terrace looking over the roofs of the Basilica and the Torre dell'Orologio,and is one of the most attractive (and, of course, expensive) one-star rooms in the city. Non-smoking. €50–140.

Al Gambero Calle dei Fabbri 4687 ☎041.522.4384, ⓦ www .locandaalgambero.com. Twenty-six-room three-star hotel in an excellent position a short distance off the north side of the Piazza; many of the rooms overlook a canal that's on the standard gondola route from the Bacino Orseolo. There's a boisterous Franco-Italian bistro on the ground floor. €70–230.

Casa Petrarca Calle delle Schiavini 4386 ☎041.520.0430, ⓔ casapetrarca@yahoo .it. A very hospitable one-star, one of the cheapest hotels within a stone's throw of the Piazza – but make sure you phone first, as it has only seven rooms, including a tiny single. No credit cards. Doubles from around €75–125.

Noemi Calle dei Fabbri 909 ☎041.523.8144, ⓦ www.hotelnoemi .com. *Noemi* is right in the thick of the action, just a minute's walk north of the Piazza, so it's hardly surprising that its prices are higher than nearly all the other one-stars. Out of season, though, it has

doubles for as little as €60. Decor is eighteenth-century Venetian and nearly all its fifteen rooms have private bathrooms. €60–200.

Orseolo Corte Zorzi 1083 ☎041.520.4827, ⓦ www.locandaorseolo .com. Friendly family-run locanda abutting the Orseolo canal, 50m north of the Piazza. Rooms are spacious and light; breakfasts substantial. Entrance is through an iron gate in Campo S. Gallo. €120–230.

San Marco: West of the Piazza

These hotels are marked on the map on pp.72–73

Ala Campo S. Maria del Giglio 2494 ☎041.520.8333, ⓦ www.hotelala.it. The 85-room three-star family-run *Ala* has spacious rooms (choose between modern and traditional Venetian) and a perfect location, on a square that opens out onto the mouth of the Canal Grande. Often has good special offers. €70–340.

Art Deco Calle delle Botteghe 2966 ☎041.277.0558, ⓦ www .locandaartdeco.com. This three-star *locanda* has a seventeenth-century palazzo setting, but the interior is strewn with 1930s and 1940s objects and the pristinely white bedrooms have modern wrought-iron furniture. Doubles from around €75–190.

Fiorita Campiello Nuovo 3457 ☎041.523.4754, ⓦ www.locandafiorita .com. Welcoming one-star with just ten rooms (and, occasionally, extra accommodation nearby), so it's crucial to book well in advance. Doubles from around €50–145.

Flora Calle Larga XXII Marzo 2283/a ☎041.520.5844, ⓦ www.hotelflora.it. This large three-star is very close to the Piazza and has a delightful inner garden. Rooms are beautifully decorated with period pieces, though some are a little cramped. €140–290.

Gritti Palace S. Maria del Giglio 2467 ☎041.794.611, ⓦ www.starwood .com/grittipalace. One of Venice's most prestigious addresses, reeking of old-regime opulence. No doubles under €300 per night, and in summer the best

suite will set you back well over €4000.
€300–1300.

Kette Piscina S. Moisè 2053
☎041.520.7766, ⊕www.hotelkette.com.
A four-star favourite with the upper-bracket
tour companies, mainly on account of its
quiet location, in an alleyway parallel to Calle
Larga XXII Marzo. In season there's nothing
under €300, but out of season prices are
much more reasonable. €140–390.

Monaco and Grand Canal Calle
Vallaresso 1325 ☎041.520.0211,
⊕www.hotelmonaco.it. The ground-
floor rooms on the waterfront side of this
famous four-star hotel (now owned by the
Benetton family) look over to the Salute
and are kitted out in full-blown olde-worlde
Venetian style, with kilos of Murano glass
and great swags of brocade. In the annexe
– the Palazzo Selvadego – you don't get
a view of the water, but the decor is in a
lighter nouveau-Mediterranean style, with
walls of plain warm colour. Prices can be
as low as €160 out of season (the website
often has very good reductions), but expect
to pay three times as much in summer. €
160–580.

Novecento Calle del Dose 2683
☎041.241.3765, ⊕www
.locandanovecento.it. Boutique-style
three-star hotel with nine individually
decorated doubles with bathrooms. Styling
is ethnic eclectic (floor cushions and Moroc-
can lamps), and there's a small courtyard
for breakfast. €140–260.

Dorsoduro

These hotels are marked on the
map on pp.80–81.

Accademia Villa Maravege Fondamenta
Bollani 1058 ☎041.521.0188, ⊕www
.pensioneaccademia.it. Once the Russian
embassy, this three-star seventeenth-century villa has a devoted following, not least
on account of its garden, which occupies
a promontory at the convergence of two
canals, with a view of a small section of the
Canal Grande. Decor is traditional Venetian
antique, with bare stone and wooden
flooring. To be sure of a room, get your
booking in at least three months ahead.
€120–280.

Agli Alboretti Rio Terrà Foscarini 884
☎041.523.0058, ⊕www.aglialboretti
.com. Friendly three-star well situated right
next to the Accademia. All rooms have a/c
and TV. €100–190.

Ca' Fóscari Calle della Frescada 3888
☎041.710.401, ⊕www
.locandacafoscari.com. Quiet, well
decorated and relaxed one-star, tucked
away in a micro-alley near S. Tomà. Just
eleven rooms (seven with bathroom), so it's
quickly booked out. €85–95.

Ca' Maria Adele Rio Terrà dei Catecumeni 111 ☎041.520.3078, ⊕www
.camariaadele.it. Five of the fourteen
rooms in this new very upmarket *locanda*
are so-called "theme rooms" – the Sala
Noir, for example, is a "voluptuous and hot"
environment in cocoa and spice tones. The
other rooms are less artfully conceived (and
€100–200 cheaper), but all are spacious
and very comfortable. €245–550.

Ca' Pisani Rio Terà Foscarini 979a
☎041.240.1411, ⊕www.capisanihotel
.it. This very glamorous 29-room four-star,
just a few metres from the Accademia, created quite a stir when it opened in 2000,
chiefly because of its high-class retro look.
Taking its cue from the style of the 1930s
and 1940s, the *Ca' Pisani* makes heavy
use of dark wood and chrome, a refreshing
break from the Renaissance and Rococo
tones that tend to prevail in Venice's upmarket establishments. €170–415.

DD 724 Ramo da Mula 724
☎041.277.0262, ⊕www.dd724.com.
In a city awash with nostalgia, the cool
high-grade modernist style of this new
boutique hotel, right by the Guggenheim,
is very welcome. It has just seven rooms,
each of them impeccably cool and luxurious
– and not a Murano chandelier in sight.
€200–250.

La Calcina Záttere ai Gesuati 780
☎041.520.6466, ⊕www.lacalcina.com.
Charismatic three-star hotel in the house
where Ruskin wrote much of *The Stones of
Venice*. From the more expensive rooms you
can gaze across to the Redentore, a church
that gave him apoplexy. All rooms are no-
smoking and have parquet floors – unusual
in Venice. No TV or minibar in the rooms– a
decision indicative of the desire to maintain

the building's character. Its restaurant (see p.90) is good too. €100–190.

Locanda San Barnaba Calle del Traghetto 2785 ☎041.241.1233, ⊛www.locanda -sanbarnaba.com. Exceptionally pleasant three-star hotel right by the Ca' Rezzonico. Well-equipped rooms – some have eighteenth-century frescoes, and one has an enormous family-size bath. €120–180.

Messner Rio Terrà dei Catacumeni 216 ☎041.522.7443, ⊛www.hotelmessner .it. In an excellent, quiet location close to the Salute vaporetto stop, the *Messner* has modern, smart rooms and is run by friendly staff. The one-star annexe round the corner past the *Alla Salute* hotel has doubles that are a little cheaper than those in the smaller but more appealing two-star main building. Doubles from around €90–145.

Pausania Fondamenta Gherardini 3942 ☎041.522.2083, ⊛www.hotelpausania .it. This quiet, comfortable and friendly three-star has an excellent location very close to San Barnaba church, just five minutes from the Accademia. Very good low-season offers. €62–250.

San Polo and Santa Croce

These hotels are marked on the map on p.94–95.

Al Gallo Calle del Forno, Santa Croce 88 ☎ 041.523.6761, ⊛www.algallo.com. Small family-run three-star, not far from the Frari, with rooms (with and without bathroom) furnished in time-honoured Venetian style. €65–115.

Alex Rio Terrà Frari, San Polo 2606 ☎041.523.1341, ⊛www.hotel alexinvenice.com. A longstanding budget travellers' favourite. No credit cards. €70–100.

Falier Salizzada S. Pantalon, Santa Croce 130 ☎041.710.882, ⊛www .hotelfalier.com. Neat, sprucely renovated little two-star, very close to San Rocco and the Frari. Doubles from around €180.

Salieri Fondamenta Minotto, Santa Croce 160 ☎041.710.035, ⊛www .hotelsalieri.com. Exceptionally friendly

one-star hotel, on a very picturesque canal-side. Rooms are light and airy. €55–160.

San Cassiano-Ca' Favretto Calle della Rosa, Santa Croce 2232 ☎041.524.1768, ⊛www.sancassiano .it. Beautiful three-star with some rooms looking across the Canal Grande towards the Ca' d'Oro. Has very helpful staff, a nice courtyard garden and a grand entrance hall. €85–390.

Sturion Calle del Sturion, San Polo 679 ☎041.523.6243, ⊛www.locandasturion .com. This immaculate eleven-room three-star has a very long pedigree – the sign of the sturgeon (*sturion*) appears in Carpaccio's *Miracle of the True Cross at the Rialto Bridge* (in the Accademia). It's on a wonderful site a few yards from the Canal Grande, close to the Rialto, but visitors with mobility difficulties should look elsewhere, as the hotel is at the top of three flights of stairs and has no lift. €60–310.

Cannaregio

These hotels are marked on the map on pp.108–109.

Abbazia Calle Priuli 68 ☎041.717.333, ⊛www.abbaziahotel.com. Occupying a former Carmelite monastery (the monks attached to the Scalzi still live in a building adjoining the hotel), the light-filled *Abbazia* provides three-star amenities without losing its air of quasi-monastic austerity. There's a delightful garden too. €70–230.

Adua Lista di Spagna 233/a ☎041.716.184, ⊛www.aduahotel .com. Thirteen-room two-star with friendly management and benign prices. One of the best hotels in this area of the city. €45–130.

Antico Doge Sottoportego Falier 5670 ☎041.241.1570, ⊛www.anticodoge .com. Located within a stone's throw of church of Santi Apostoli, this very comfortable *locanda* occupies part of the palace that once belonged to the disgraced doge Marin Falier. €100–350.

Bernardi Semenzato Calle dell'Oca 4366 ☎041.522.7257, ⊛www.hotelbernardi .com. Very well-priced two-star in a prime location (in a tiny alleyway close to Campo

SS Apostoli), with immensely helpful owners who speak excellent English. Has five singles for as little as €40 (with shared bathroom). €65–115.

Casa Martini Rio Terrà S. Leonardo 1314 ☎041.717.512, ⊚www .casamartini.it. Delightful small hotel near the Cannaregio canal. Nine pleasantly furnished a/c rooms, with breakfast terrace at the back and kitchen for guests' use. €90–160.

Del Ghetto Campo del Ghetto Novo 2892 ☎041.275.9292, ⊚www .locandadelghetto.net. Friendly nine-room locanda in the heart of the Ghetto. Well-equipped a/c rooms have beautiful features, including wooden floors and old beams. Two rooms have a small balcony. Kosher breakfast. Doubles from around €80–220.

Giorgione Calle Larga dei Proverbi 4587 ☎041.522.5810, ⊚www.hotelgiorgione .com. High-class four-star hotel not far from the Rialto bridge, with a very personal touch – it has been run by the same family for generations. Non-smoking floor, quiet courtyard, pool table, free internet access and 76 well-equipped rooms, including rooms for disabled visitors. Free tea and coffee served in lounge in the afternoon. €100–400.

Locanda Ai Santi Apostoli Strada Nova 4391a ☎041.521.2612, ⊚www.locandasantiapostoli.com. Occupying the top floor of a palazzo opposite the Rialto market, this ten-room three-star is one of the pricier locande, but there aren't many better rooms in this price than the pair overlooking the Canal Grande – and if you want one of these, you'll need to get your request in early. €100–280.

Locanda Leon Bianco Corte Leon Bianco 5629 ☎041.523.3572, ⊚www .leonbianco.it. Friendly and charming three-star in a superb location not far from the Rialto bridge, tucked away beside the decaying Ca' da Mosto. Only eight rooms, but three of them overlook the Canal Grande and four of the others are spacious and tastefully furnished in eighteenth-century style – one even has a huge fresco in the mode of Giambattista Tiepolo. A gem of a place. €90–200.

Novo Calle dei Preti 4529 ☎041.241.1496, ⊚www.locandanovo .it. Popular locanda in a lovingly refurbished palazzo near Santi Apostoli. Ten large, well-furnished rooms, some with a/c. €90–150.

Palazzo Abadessa Calle Priuli 4011 ☎041.241.3784, ⊚www.abadessa .com. This residenza d'epoca is a meticulously restored palazzo behind the church of Santa Sofia; all twelve of its bedrooms (some of them huge) are discreetly furnished with genuine antiques, and there's a lovely secluded garden as well. €175–300.

Villa Rosa Calle della Misericordia 389 ☎041.716.569, ⊚www.villarosahotel .com. Clean and fairly large one-star; the rooms here have a/c and private bathrooms – the best even have a small balcony. There is a large terrace at the back for breakfast. €65–135.

Central Castello

These hotels are marked on the map on p.119.

Al Leon Campo SS Filippo e Giacomo 4270 ☎041.277.0393, ⊚www .hotelalleon.com. Friendly locanda very close to the Piazza, with nine pleasantly furnished a/c rooms – not big, but well-equipped. €90–180.

Canada Campo S. Lio 5659 ☎041.522.9912, ⊕041.523.5852. Well-kept and friendly second-floor two-star; book well in advance for the room with a roof terrace. Other rooms are perfectly comfortable, if unremarkable. €50–175.

Caneva Corte Rubbi 5515 ☎041.522.8118, ⊚www.hotelcaneva .com. A well-appointed and peaceful one-star tucked away behind the church of Santa Maria della Fava, close to Campo S. Bartolomeo. Most of the 23 rooms have a/c and private bathroom. €50–110.

Casa Querini Campo S. Giovanni Novo 4388 ☎041.241.1294, ⊚www .locandaquerini.com. Friendly small locanda occupying parts of two houses in a quiet courtyard near the Piazza. Eleven smallish but nicely furnished a/c rooms. €100–200.

Casa Verardo Calle della Chiesa 4765 ☎041.528.6127, ⊛www.casaverardo.it. Very fine, well-refurbished three-star hotel just a couple of minutes from San Marco and Campo Santa Maria Formosa. Twenty very well-equipped rooms with a breakfast terrace downstairs, a sun lounge at the top and another terrace attached to the priciest of the rooms. €90–360.

Danieli Riva degli Schiavoni 4196 ☎041.522.6480, ⊛www.luxury collection.com/danieli. No longer the most expensive hotel in Venice (the *Cipriani* has that title), but no other place can compete with the glamour of the *Danieli*. Balzac stayed here, as did George Sand, Wagner and Dickens. This magnificent Gothic palazzo affords just about the most sybaritic hotel experience on the continent – provided you book a room in the old part of the building, not the modern extension. €600–1300.

Doni Fondamenta del Vin 4656 ☎041.522.4267, ⊛www.albergodoni .it. A cosy one-star near San Zaccaria, and most of the thirteen rooms look over the Rio del Vin or a courtyard. Only six of the rooms have a private bathroom. Room 8 is special for its ceiling fresco. €80–120.

Paganelli Riva degli Schiavoni 4687 ☎041.522.4324, ⊛www.hotelpaganelli .com. This three-star is a great place to stay, as long as you get one of the rooms on the lagoon side – the ones in the annexe look onto S. Zaccaria, which is a nice enough view, but not really in the same league. Very good out-of-season rates. €80–240.

Scandinavia Campo S. Maria Formosa 5240 ☎041.522.3507, ⊛www .scandinaviahotel.com. Sizeable and comfortable three-star on one of the city's most lively and spacious squares. Decorated mainly in eighteenth-century style (ie lots of Murano glass and floral motifs), it has an unusually wide variety of accommodation, ranging from large suites to rooms with private but not en-suite bathroom. Huge reductions in the quiet months. €60–310.

Eastern Castello

These hotels are marked on the map on pp.128–129.

Casa Linger Salizzada S. Antonin 3541 ☎041.528.5920, ⊛www.hotelcasalinger .com. Well off the tourist rat-run, this one-star is a decent budget option, as long as you don't mind the climb to the front door – it's at the top of a very steep staircase. Good-sized rooms with and without bathroom. €40–130.

Gabrielli Sandwirth Riva degli Schiavoni 4110 ☎041.523.1580, ⊛www.hotel gabrielli.it. A converted Gothic palace, with a lovely courtyard. Four-star comfort and *Danieli*-style views across the Bacino di San Marco for around a third of the price of the *Danieli*. €150–450.

La Residenza Campo Bandiera e Moro 3608 ☎041.528.5315, ⊛www .venicelaresidenza.com. This fourteenth-century palazzo is a low-budget gem (in Venetian terms), occupying much of one side of a tranquil square just off the main waterfront. It was once a tad pricier than the average two-star, but the rest of the pack have raised their tariffs more in recent years, making *La Residenza* a top choice. The recently refurbished rooms are spacious (rare at this price) and elegant. €80–160.

Bed & Breakfast

The Italian tourism authorities define a **bed and breakfast** as an establishment in a private dwelling in which a maximum of three bedrooms are available to paying guests, with a mini-mum of one shared bathroom for guests' exclusive use. As is always the case however, nomenclature is not straightforward, as some some larger guesthouses like to call themselves B&Bs, because they think the label gives them a touch of anglophone chic. The places listed below are all officially registered B&Bs; guesthouses are included in the hotel listings. The tourist office has lists of around 150 officially registered B&Bs, and the number is growing with each year . Some of these – as you may expect in a city where you could charge €100 for the privilege of sleeping on a mattress in the attic – are not terribly attractive. Our selection is taken from those whose rooms are viewable online, with ★★ marking our top choices. For full listings of Venice's B&Bs, go to www.turismovenezia.it; Ⓦwww.bed-and-breakfast.it is another useful resource.

SAN MARCO

A Le Boteghe Calle delle Botteghe 3438 Ⓦwww.aleboteghe.it €110
Ca' del Pozzo Calle Lavezzera 2612 Ⓦwww.cadelpozzo.com €150–180
Ca' Moroni Campo Sant'Angelo 3824 Ⓦwww.camoroni.it €80–130
Casa de' Uscoli Campo Pisani S. Marco 2818 Ⓦwww.casadeuscoli.com E180 ★★
Palazzo Duodo Gregolin Ramo Duodo 1014 Ⓦwww.palazzoduodo.com €130–180 ★★
Room in Venice Calle S. Antonio 4114a Ⓦwww.roominvenice.com €50–100

DORSODURO

Ai Mendicoli Campiello Tron 1902 Ⓦwww.aimendicoli.com €90–130
Almaviva House Fondamenta delle Romite 1348 Ⓦwww.palazzopompeo.com €180 ★★
Ca' Arzere Corte Maggiore 2314 Ⓦwww.bbveneziarzere.com €80–130
Ca' Turelli Fondamenta di Borgo 1162 Ⓦwww.caturelli.it €100-150 ★★
Corte Contarini Corte Contarini 3488r Ⓦwww.cortecontarini.it €70–90
Fujiyama Calle Lungo S. Barnabà 2727a Ⓦwww.bedandbreakfast-fujiyama.it €80–140 ★★
La Colonna Gotica Campo Angelo Raffaele 1710 Ⓦwww.veneziabedandbreakfast.it €75–120
Palazzo dal Carlo Fondamenta di Borgo 1163 Ⓦwww.palazzodalcarlo.com €140–150 ★★

SAN POLO and SANTA CROCE

Al Campaniel Calle del Campaniel 2889 Ⓦwww.alcampaniel.com €55–110
Al Campiello dei Meloni Campiello dei Meloni 1419a Ⓦwww.ciprea.info €50–85
Ca' Angeli Calle del Traghetto della Madoneta 1434 Ⓦwww.caangeli.it €**110–300**
Corte 1321 Campiello Ca' Bernardi Ⓦwww.cabernardi.it €100–220

CANNAREGIO

Al Palazzetto Calle delle Vele 4057 Ⓦwww.guesthouse.it €90–200 ★★
Al Saor Ca' d'Oro Calle Zotti 3904a Ⓦwww.alsaor.com €80–100 ★★
At Home a Palazzo Calle Priuli 3764 Ⓦwww.athomeapalazzo.com €130–200
Ca' Pier Calle Bembo 4357 Ⓦwww.capier.com €45–150 ★★

CASTELLO

Ai Greci Calle del Magazen 3338 Ⓦwww.aigreci.com €80–160 ★★
Ca' Furlan alla Croce di Malta Corte S. Giovanni di Malta 3257 Ⓦwww.cafurlan.it €70–170
Campiello Santa Giustina Calle Due Porte 6499 Ⓦwww.campiellogiustina.com €60–110
Ciprea Calle Corera 986c Ⓦwww.ciprea.info €60–110
Gli Angeli Campo della Tana 2161 Ⓦwww.gliangeli.net €85–170
San Marco Fondamenta S. Giorgio degli Schiavoni 3385 ℡041.522.7589, Ⓦwww.realvenice.it/smarco /€80–130 ★★

GIUDECCA

Casa Eden Corte Mosto 25 Ⓦwww.casaeden.it €70–110 ★★
Casa Genoveffa Calle del Forno 472 Ⓦwww.casagenoveffa.com €60-180★★
Corte Grande dei Sette Camini Corte Grande 501 Ⓦwww.cortegrandi.it €130–180★★

Apartments

The very high cost of hotel rooms in Venice makes self-catering an attractive option – for the price of a week in a cramped double room in a three-star hotel you could book yourself a two-bedroomed apartment right in the centre of the city. Many package holiday companies have a few Venetian apartments in their brochures, and the tourist office in Venice has an ever-expanding list of landlords on its books, who charge anything between €200 and €4000 per week: these properties can be found through www.turismovenezia.it. In addition, the following sites are worth checking out.

Holiday Rentals ⓦ www.holiday-rentals .com. This site – which puts you in touch directly with the owners – features over seventy properties in Venice (with more in the Veneto), from under £400pw.

Italian Breaks ⓦ www.italianbreaks .com. This company has a selection of a couple of dozen apartments in Venice, ranging from a one-bed place near the Fondamente Nuove to a four-bedroomed apartment with views of the Canal Grande.

Venetian Apartments ⓦ www.venice -rentals.com. Venetian Apartments offers more than a hundred apartments in the city, ranging from studios at around €825 per week, through one, two, three- and four-bedroomed apartments to extraordinarily sumptuous palazzi on the Canal Grande that will set you back around €11,000. The properties are immaculately maintained, and the agency provides very friendly back-up in Venice itself. It also has an exemplary website, with detailed maps showing the location of each apartment, photographs of virtually every room in each property, ground plans and full rental details.

Venice Apartment ⓦ www .veniceapartment.com. An Italian website with more than a hundred properties on its books.

VeniceApartmentsOrg ⓦ www.venice apartments.org. There are dozens of apartments on the site – and even a ten-berth boat on the Brenta canal.

Visit Venice ⓦ www.visitvenice.co.uk. Two meticulously maintained small houses – Casa Tre Archi and Casa Battello – in the Ghetto district of Cannaregio; they are remarkably good value, and the owners could not be more helpful.

Hostels

Venice has a large HI hostel and a few hostel-like establishments run by religious foundations, which are generally available to tourists during the university's summer vacation – during term time they double as student accommodation.

Domus Ciliota Calle delle Muneghe, S. Marco 2976 ⓣ041.520.4888, ⓦ www .ciliota.it; map on pp.72–73. Welcoming

but expensive mixed hostel-style accommodation, close to Campo S. Stefano. Open mid-June to mid-Sept. Singles from €70, doubles from €100.

Domus Civica Calle Campazzo, S. Polo 3082 ⓣ041.721.103; map on pp.94–95. A student house in winter, open to travellers from mid-June to Sept. Most rooms are double with running water; showers free; no breakfast; 11.30pm curfew. €30 per night, with reductions for ISIC and Rolling Venice Card holders.

Foresteria Valdese **S. Maria Formosa, Castello 5170** ☎**041.528.6797,** ⓦ**www .diaconiavaldese.org; map on pp.118– 119.** Run by Waldensians, this hostel is installed in a wonderful palazzo at the end of Calle Lunga S. Maria Formosa, with flaking frescoes in the rooms, a large salon and cheap internet access. It has several large dorms, plus bedrooms that can accommodate up to eight people. Reservations by phone only; dorm beds cannot be booked in advance, except by groups. Registration 9am–1pm & 6–8pm. Prices average out at around €22 per night.

Ostello Santa Fosca **S. Maria dei Servi, Cannaregio 2372,** ☎**041.715.733,** ⓦ**www.santafosca.com; map on pp.108–109.** Student-run hostel in an atmospheric former Servite convent in a quiet part of Cannaregio, with dorm beds and double rooms, all with shared bathrooms. Check-in 5–8pm; 12.30pm curfew. €20 per person on average. They take bookings one week ahead only, and only by phone; it's essential to book in summer.

Ostello Venezia **Fondamenta delle Zitelle, Giudecca 86** ☎**041.523.8211;** ⓔ**vehostel@tin.it.** The city's HI hostel occupies a superb location looking over to San Marco, but it's run with a certain briskness. Registration opens at 1.30pm in summer and 4pm in winter. Curfew at 11.30pm, chucking-out time 9.30am. Gets so busy in July and August that written reservations must be made by April; written reservations are required all year. Breakfast and sheets included in the price – but remember to add the expense of the boat over to Giudecca (the nearest stop is Zitelle). No kitchen, but full (and good) meals for around €10. From €18.50 per dorm bed, breakfast included; HI card necessary, but you can join on the spot.

Essentials

Arrival

Millions of visitors pour into Venice each year, most of them funnelled through Venice's Marco Polo airport, on the outskirts of Venice itself, or through Treviso, 30km inland. Arriving by train and coach is painless – but driving into Venice is unmitigated hell in summer.

By air

Most **scheduled** flights and some charters arrive at the recently enlarged and smartened **Marco Polo**, around 7km north of Venice, on the edge of the lagoon. If you're on a package holiday the cost of transport to the city centre, either by land or by water, might already be covered. If it's not, the most inexpensive way into town is to take one of the two road-going **bus services** to the terminal at Piazzale Roma: the ATVO (*Azienda Trasporti Veneto Orientale*) coach, which departs every half-hour and takes around twenty minutes (€3), or the ACTV (*Azienda del Consorzio Trasporti Veneziano*; ✆ www.actv.it) bus #5/5D, which is equally frequent, usually takes just five minutes longer (it's a local bus service, so it picks up and puts down passengers between the airport and Piazzale Roma), and costs €2. If you'd prefer to approach the city by water, you could take one of the Alilaguna **water-buses**, which operate on three routes: Murano (€6) – Lido – Arsenale – San Marco – Záttere (all €11; service hourly 6.15am–12.15am; journey 1hr to San Marco); Murano – Fondamente Nove (€6) – Lido – San Zaccaria – San Marco (hourly 9.45am–11.45pm); and directly to San Zaccaria and then San Marco (hourly 9.30am–5.30pm). **Ticket offices** for water-buses and land buses are in the arrivals hall; in addition to single tickets,

you can also get ACTV passes and Venice Cards here (see p.174) – a wise investment for almost all visitors. Note that ACTV passes are not valid on the Alilaguna service nor on the ATVO bus, but a version of the Venice Card can be used on Alilaguna's boats. Land buses and taxis depart from immediately outside the arrivals hall; a free shuttle bus takes you to the Alilaguna boats and water-taxis.

The most luxurious mode of transport is a **water-taxi**. The drivers tout for business in and around the arrivals hall, and will charge in the region of €90 to San Marco, for up to six people. Ordinary **car-taxis** are ranked outside the arrivals hall, and cost about €30 to Piazzale Roma.

Treviso airport is used chiefly by **charter** companies, some of which provide a free bus link from the airport into Venice. Ryanair's twice-daily flights use Treviso too, and are met by an ATVO bus service to Venice; the fare is €5 single and the journey takes 1hr 10min. Otherwise, take the #6 bus from right outside the arrivals building into Treviso (20min), from where there are very frequent bus and train connections to Venice. Tickets are best bought before you get onto the bus, from the bar across the road; if you buy them from the driver they cost almost twice as much.

By road and rail

Arriving by **train**, **coach or bus**, you simply get off at the end of the line. The **Piazzale Roma** bus station and **Santa Lucia** train station (don't get off at Venezia Mestre, which is the last stop on the mainland) are just five minutes' walk from each other at the top of the Canal Grande. For details of **left-luggage** facilities, see p.181.

Information

The main **tourist office** – known as the **Venice Pavilion** – occupies the Palazzina del Santi, on the west side of the Giardinetti Reali, within a minute of the Piazza San Marco (daily 10am–6pm; ☎041.529.8711, ⓦ www.turismovenezia .it); smaller offices operate at Calle dell'Ascensione 71/f, in the corner of the Piazza's arcades (daily 9am–3.30pm; ☎041.520.8740), the train station (daily 8am–6.30pm; ☎041.529.8727), in the airport arrivals area (Mon–Sat 9.30am– 7.30pm; ☎041.541.5887), at the multistorey car park at Piazzale Roma (daily 9.30am–6.30pm; ☎041.529.8746), and on the Lido at Gran Viale S.M. Elisabetta 6 (June–Sept daily 9.30am–12.30pm & 3.30–6pm; ☎041.526.5721).

These offices produce free listings of museums, exhibitions and concerts. The English–Italian **magazine** *Un Ospite di Venezia* (ⓦ www.unospitedivenezia .it), produced fortnightly in summer and monthly in winter, gives slightly fuller information on special events, plus extras such as vaporetto timetables; it's free from the receptions of many four- and five-star hotels. The fullest source of information, though, is *VE: News* (€2.20), which is published on the first day of each month and is sold at newsstands all over the city; it has good coverage of exhibitions, cultural events, bars and restaurants, with a fair amount of text presented in English as well as Italian.

The Venice and Rolling Venice cards

Active sightseers should consider buying a **Venice Card**, which comes in two forms and is valid for either one, three or seven days, with a discount for the under-30s. The **blue** card (1-day €17, €15 with discount; 3-day €34/€30; 7-day €52/€47) gives unlimited use of all ACTV public transport and free access to some public toilets, most usefully those at Piazzale Roma, Campo San Bartolomeo, the Piazza (off the west side) and the Giardini Reali (by the tourist office). The **orange** card (1-day €29/€22; 3-day €54/€45; 7-day €76/€67) accords the same benefits as the blue card and also gives free access to all the museums covered by the Museum Pass and the Chorus Pass (see p.178). For a €20 supplement you can buy a version of the blue and orange cards that's valid on Alilaguna services to and from the airport. Note that kids under 6 get free museum entrance but only under-4s get free travel on public transport – so for 4- and 5-year-olds an orange card is a pointless investment.

You can buy Venice Cards from the tourist offices, the VeLa/ACTV offices at the airport, train station and Piazzale Roma, and the Alilaguna desk at the airport. Alternatively, you can order the card a minimum of 48 hours in advance online at ⓦ www.venicecard.it (which gives a discount of up to €2.50) or by calling ☎899.909.090 (within Italy – it's a free number) or ☎00.39.041.2424 (from abroad). You will be given a code number which you will need to present when you turn up to collect your ticket from any of the offices listed above.

If you are aged between 14 and 29, you are eligible for a **Rolling Venice** card, which entitles you to discounts at some shops, restaurants, hostels, campsites, museums, concerts and exhibitions, plus a discount on the 72-hour ACTV travel pass; details are given in a leaflet that comes with the card. The card costs €5, is valid until the end of the year in which it is bought, and is worth buying if you are in town for at least a week and aim to make the most of every minute. The tourist offices and VeLa/ACTV offices issue it, on production of a passport or similar ID.

City transport

With the exceptions of the #1 and #82 and a couple of other peak-hours services, the water-buses skirt the city centre, connecting points on the periphery and the outer islands. In many cases the speediest way of getting around is **on foot**. Routes between major sights are sometimes tortuous but distances are short (you can cross the whole city in an hour), and once you've got your general bearings you'll find that navigation is not as daunting as it seems at first. Yellow signs posted high up on streetcorners all over central Venice indicate the main routes to San Marco, Ferrovia (train station) and Rialto.

Water-buses

There are two basic types of boat: the **vaporetti**, which are the lumbering workhorses used on the Canal Grande services (#1 and #82) and other heavily used routes; and the **motoscafi**, which are smaller vessels employed on routes where the volume of traffic isn't as great (notably the two "circular routes" – #41/42 and #51/52).

The standard **fare** for non-residents is €5 for a single journey; the ticket is valid for sixty minutes. Should you have more than one piece of large luggage, you're supposed to pay €5 per additional item. Children under 4 travel free on all water-buses. **Tickets** are available from most landing stages, *tabacchi*, shops displaying the ACTV sign, tourist offices and the VeLa/ACTV office at Piazzale Roma (daily: summer 6am–midnight; winter 6am–8pm). In the remoter parts of the city you may not be able to find anywhere to buy a ticket, particularly after working hours, when the booths at the landing stages tend to close down; tickets can be bought on board at the standard price, as long as you ask the attendant as soon as you get on board; if you delay, you could be liable for a €30 spot-fine on top of the fare.

Unless you intend to walk all day, you'll almost certainly save money by buying some sort of **travel card** as soon as you arrive. ACTV produces a **24-hour** ticket (€12) and a **72-hour** ticket (€25), which can be used on all ACTV services within Venice (including ACTV land buses from the airport). For seven days of unrestricted travel, you have to buy a Venice Card (see opposite).

If you buy one of these unrestricted travel tickets at Piazzale Roma, the train station, San Zaccaria or San Marco, it will in all likelihood be automatically **validated** with a time-stamp; the same goes for ordinary tickets. When using a **non-validated** ticket you must validate it before embarking, by inserting it into one of the machines at the entrance to the vaporetto stop or on board the bus (the machines are painted orange); the ticket is valid from that moment, and you need to validate it just once.

Water-bus services

What follows is a run-through of the **water-bus routes** that visitors are most likely to find useful; a fully comprehensive (and free) timetable can usually be picked up at the major vaporetto stops: Piazzale Roma, Ferrovia, San Marco, San Zaccaria, Accademia, Fondamente Nove. Be warned that so many services call at San Marco, San Zaccaria, Rialto and the train station that the stops at these points are spread out over a long stretch of waterfront, so you might have to walk past several stops before finding the one you need. Note that the main San Marco stop is also known as San Marco Vallaresso, or plain Vallaresso, and that the San Zaccaria stop is as close to the Basilica as is the Vallaresso stop.

#1

The slowest of the water-buses, and the one you'll use most often. It starts at Piazzale Roma, calls at every stop on the Canal Grande except San Samuele, works its way along the San Marco waterfront to Sant'Elena, then goes over to the Lido. The #1 runs every 20min between 5 and 6.30am, every 10min between 6.30am and 9.45pm, and every 20min between 9.45 and 11.45pm. For the night service, see #N below.

#3

The quickest service down the Canal Grande, running every 20min from Tronchetto to San Marco between 8.30am and 12.50pm, calling at Piazzale Roma, Ferrovia, San Samuele and Accademia en route.

#82

The #82 is in effect a speeded-up version of the #1, as it makes fewer stops on the Canal Grande. Its clockwise route takes it from San Zaccaria to San Giorgio Maggiore, Giudecca (Zitelle, Redentore and Palanca), Zàttere, San Basilio, Sacca Fisola, Tronchetto, Piazzale Roma, the train station, then down the Canal Grande (usually calling at Rialto, Sant'Angelo, San Tomà, San Samuele and Accademia; from around 4–8pm it calls at San Marcuola) to San Marco (Vallaresso); the anti-clockwise version calls at the same stops. From Monday to Friday the #82 runs along most of the route (in both directions) every 10min from 6am to 8.30pm, then every 20min until 11pm, but for the section between Rialto and San Marco the bus runs only every 20min through the day and is even less frequent before 8am and after 8.30pm; at weekends the #82 runs every 20min for the whole route. In summer the #82 is extended from San Zaccaria to the Lido. For the night service see #N below.

#41/42

The circular service, running right round the core of Venice, with a short detour at the northern end to San Michele and Murano. The #41 travels anticlockwise, the #42 clockwise and both run every 20min from 6.30am until around 8pm; after that, the #41/42 together act as a shuttle service between Murano and Fondamente Nove, running every 20min until around 11.30pm.

#51/52

Similar to the #41/42, this route also circles Venice, but heads out to the Lido (rather than Murano) at the easternmost end of the circle. The #51 runs anticlockwise, the #52 clockwise, and both run fast through the Giudecca canal, stopping only at Zàttere and Santa Marta between San Zaccaria and

Piazzale Roma. Both run every 20min for most of the day. In the early morning and late evening (4.30–6am & 8.30–11pm) the #51 doesn't do a complete lap of the city – instead it departs every 20min from Fondamenta Nove and proceeds via the train station to the Lido, where it terminates; similarly, from about 8–11pm the #52 (which starts operating at 6am) shuttles between the Lido and Fondamente Nove in the opposite direction, and from 11pm to around 12.20am goes no farther than the train station.

#LN

For most of the day the "Laguna Nord" runs every half-hour from Fondamente Nove (approximately hourly from 7.40pm to 11.20pm), calling first at Murano-Faro before heading on to Mazzorbo, Burano (from where there is a connecting half-hourly #T shuttle to Torcello), Treporti, Punta Sabbioni, the Lido and San Zaccaria (the Pietà stop); it runs with the same frequency in the opposite direction.

#DM

From around 8am to 6pm the "Diretto Murano" runs from Tronchetto via Piazzale Roma and Ferrovia to Murano, where it always calls at Colonna and Museo, and often at other Murano stops too.

#N

This night service (11.30pm–4.30am) is a selective fusion of the #1 and #82 routes, running from the Lido to Giardini, San Zaccaria, San Marco (Vallaresso), Canal Grande (Accademia, San Samuele, San Tomà, Rialto, Ca' d'Oro, San Stae, San Marcuola), train station, Piazzale Roma, Tronchetto, Sacca Fisola, San Basilio, Zàttere, Giudecca (Palanca, Redentore and Zitelle), San Giorgio and San Zaccaria – and vice versa. It runs along the whole of the route in both directions roughly every 30min, and along the Rialto to Tronchetto part every 20min. Another night service connects Venice with Murano and Burano, running to and from Fondamente Nove every 30min between midnight and 4am.

Traghetti

Costing just 50 cents, **traghetti** (gondola ferries) are the only cheap way of getting a ride on a gondola, albeit a stripped-down version, with none of the *trimmings* and no padded seats – it's *de rigueur* to stand in the traghetto gondolas. The gondola traghetti across the Canal Grande are as follows; in the **winter** months it's common for traghetti services to be suspended.

Santa Maria del Giglio–Salute (Mon–Sat 9am–7pm)

Ca' Rezzonico–San Samuele (Mon–Sat 7.40am–1.20pm)

San Tomà–Santo Stefano (Mon–Sat 7am–8.50pm, Sun 8am–7.50pm)

Riva del Carbon–Riva del Vin (near Rialto, Mon–Sat 8am–2pm)

Santa Sofia–Rialto (Mon–Sat 7am–8.50pm, Sun 8am–7.50pm)

San Marcuola–Fondaco dei Turchi (Mon–Sat 7.30am–1.30pm)

Gondolas

The **gondola**, once Venice's chief form of transport, has become an adjunct of the tourist industry and the city's biggest cliché. That said, the gondola is an astonishingly graceful craft, perfectly designed for negotiating the tortuous canals, and an hour's slow voyage through the city can give you a wholly new perspective on the place. To hire one costs €73 per fifty minutes for up to six passengers, rising to €91 between 8pm and 8am; you pay an extra €37 for every additional 25 minutes, or €47 from 8pm to 8am. Further hefty surcharges will be levied should you require the services

of an on-board accordionist or tenor – and a surprising number of people do, despite the strangulated voices and hackneyed repertoire of most of the aquatic Carusos. Even though the tariff is set by the local authorities, it's been known for some gondoliers to try to extort even higher rates than these – if you do decide to go for a ride, establish the charge before setting off.

Taxis

Venice's **water-taxis** are sleek and speedy vehicles that can penetrate all but the shallowest of the city's canals. Unfortunately their use is confined to all but the owners of the deepest pockets, for they are possibly the most expensive form of taxi in Western Europe: the clock starts at €8.70 and goes up €1.30 every minute. All sorts of additional surcharges are levied as well – €1.60 for each extra person if there are more than four people in the party; €1.50 for each piece of luggage over 50cm long; €5.50 for a ride between 10pm and 7am. There are three ways of getting a taxi: go to one of the main stands (in front of the Piazzetta and at the airport), find one in the process of disgorging its passengers or call one by phone (☎041.522.2303 or 041.723.112). If you phone for one, you'll pay a surcharge of €6.

Museums and monuments

In an attempt to make sure that tourists go to see more than just the big central monuments, a couple of **Museum Cards** have been introduced for the city's civic museums. The card for **I Musei di Piazza San Marco**, costing €12 (€6.50 for ages 6–14, students under 30, EU

citizens over 65 and Rolling Venice Card holders), allows you to visit the Palazzo Ducale, Museo Correr, Museo Archeologico and the Biblioteca Marciana. The **Museum Pass**, costing €18/12, covers all the museums listed above, plus Ca' Rezzonico, Casa Goldoni, Palazzo

Mocenigo, Museo Fortuny, Ca' Pésaro (the modern art and oriental museums), the Museo del Merletto (Burano) and the Museo del Vetro (Murano). Passes are valid for six months, allow one visit to each attraction, and are available from any of the participating museums. The **Musei di Piazza San Marco** can only be visited with a Museum Card; at the other places you have the option of paying an entry charge just for that attraction. The internet site is Ⓦwww .museicivicveneziani.it. Note also that the orange version of the Venice Card (see box on p.174) covers all of the museums covered by the Museum Pass, and that accompanied disabled people have free access to all of these museums. There is also a combined ticket for the city's **state museums** (the Accademia, Ca' d'Oro and Museo Orientale), costing €11/5.50.

Sixteen churches are now part of the ever-expanding **Chorus Pass** scheme (Ⓦ www.chorusvenezia.org), whereby an €8 ticket allows one visit to each of the churches over a one-year period. All of the proceeds from the scheme are ploughed back into the maintenance of the member churches. The individual entrance fee at each of the participating churches is €2.50, and all the churches (except for the Frari) observe the same opening hours: Monday to Saturday 10am to 5pm. The churches involved are: the Frari (Mon–Sat 9am–6pm, Sun 1–6pm); the Gesuati; Madonna dell'Orto; the Redentore; San Giacomo dell'Orio; San Giobbe; San Giovanni Elemosinario; San Pietro di Castello; San Polo; San Sebastiano; San Stae; Sant'Alvise; Santa Maria dei Miracoli; Santa Maria del Giglio; Santa Maria Formosa; Santo Stefano. The Chorus Pass is available at all of these churches; the orange Venice Card gives free admission to all of them.

Festivals and special events

As recently as just one generation ago Venice was a night city, where the residents of each parish set out tables on the street at the flimsiest excuse. Nowadays, with the pavements overrun by outsiders, the social life of the Venetians is more of an indoor business – a restaurant meal or a drink with friends might feature in most people's diary for the week, and a conversational stroll is certainly a favourite Venetian pastime, but home entertainment takes up most time and energy. That said, Venice's calendar of special events is pretty impressive, with the Carnevale, the Film Festival and the Biennale ranking among the continent's hottest dates.

The Film Festival

The Venice Film Festival, founded in 1932, is the world's oldest and the most important in Europe after Cannes. The eleven-day event takes place on the Lido every year in **late August and/or early September**. Posters advertising the Festival's schedule appear weeks in advance, and the tourist office will have the Festival programme a fair time before the event, as will the two cinemas where the films are shown – the **Palazzo del Cinemà** on Lungomare G. Marconi and the neighbouring **PalaGalileo**. Tickets are available to the general public, but you have to go along and queue for them at the PalaGalileo on the day before the performance. Any remaining tickets are sold off at PalaGalileo one hour before the screening, but nearly all shows are sold out well before then. For more information go to **W** www.labiennale.org.

The Biennale

The Venice Biennale, Europe's most glamorous international forum for contemporary art, was first held in 1895 as the city's contribution to the celebrations for the silver wedding anniversary of King Umberto I and Margherita of Savoy, and is now held **every odd-numbered year from June to November**. The main site is in the Giardini Pubblici, where there are permanent pavilions for about forty countries plus space for a thematic international exhibition. This central part of the Biennale is supplemented by exhibitions in larger venues all over the city, such as the salt warehouses on the Zàttere or the colossal Corderie. In addition, smaller sites throughout the city – including the streets and parks – host fringe exhibitions, installations and performances, particularly in the opening weeks. Some pavilions and other venues are used in even-numbered years for an independent Biennale for **architecture**. Information on the Biennale is available at **W** www.labiennale.org.

Carnevale

John Evelyn wrote of the 1646 Carnevale: "all the world was in Venice to see the folly and madness . . . the women, men and persons of all conditions disguising themselves in antique dresses, & extravagant Musique & a thousand gambols." Not much is different in today's Carnevale, for which people arrive in such numbers that the causeway from the mainland has sometimes had to be closed because the city has been too packed. Originating as a communal party prior to the abstemious rigours of Lent, Carnevale takes place over the **ten days leading up to Lent**, finishing on Shrove Tuesday with a masked ball for the glitterati, and dancing in the Piazza for the plebs. During the day people don costumes and go down to the Piazza to be photographed; parents dress up their kids; businessmen can be seen doing their shopping in the classic white mask, black cloak and tricorne hat. In the evening some congregate in the remoter squares, while those who have spent hundreds of euros on their costumes install themselves in the windows of *Florian*'s and pose for a while. But you don't need to spend money or try to be "traditional" in your disguise: a simple black outfit and a painted face is enough to transform you from a spectator into a participant.

La Sensa and Vogalonga

The feast of La Sensa happens in May on the **Sunday after Ascension Day** – the latter being the day on which the doge enacted the wedding of Venice to the sea (see p.154). The ritual has recently been revived – a distinctly feeble procession which ends with the mayor and a gang of other dignitaries getting into a present-day approximation of the *Bucintoro* (the state barge) and sailing off to the Lido. A gondola regatta follows the ceremony, but far more spectacular is the Vogalonga (long row), which is held on the same day. Established in 1974 as a protest against the excessive number of motorboats on the canals, the *Vogalonga* is now open to any crew in any class of rowing boat, and covers a 32-kilometre course from the Bacino di San Marco out to Burano and back; the competitors set off at 8.30am and arrive at the bottom of the Canal Grande anywhere between about 11am and 3pm.

Festa del Redentore

The Festa del Redentore is one of Venice's plague-related festivals, marking the end of the epidemic of 1576. Celebrated on the **third Sunday in July**, the day is centred on Palladio's church of the Redentore, which was built by way of thanksgiving for the city's escape. A bridge of boats is strung across the

Giudecca canal to allow the faithful to walk over to the church, and on the Saturday night hundreds of people row out for a picnic on the water. The night ends with a grand fireworks display, after which it's traditional to row to the Lido for the sunrise.

The Regata Storica

Held on the **first Sunday in September**, the Regata Storica is the annual trial of strength and skill for the city's gondoliers and other expert rowers. It starts with a procession of richly decorated historic craft along the Canal Grande course, their crews all decked out in period dress, followed by a series of races right up the canal. Re-enacting the return of Caterina Cornaro to her native city in 1489 (see p.65), the opening parade is a spectacular affair, and the races attract a sizeable (and partisan) crowd. The first

race of the day is for young rowers in two-oared *pupparini*; the women's race comes next, and then it's the big one – the men's race, in specialized racing gondolas called *gondolini*.

La Salute

Named after the church of the Salute, the Festa della Salute is a reminder of the plague of 1630–31, which killed one third of the population of the lagoon. The church was built in thanks for deliverance from the outbreak, and every **November 21** since then the Venetians have processed over a pontoon bridge across the Canal Grande to give thanks for their good health, or to pray for sick friends and relatives. It offers the only chance to see the church as it was designed to be seen – with its main doors open and hundreds of people milling up and down the steps.

Directory

ACTV enquiries Piazzale Roma, daily 7.30am–8pm; English-language information from Hello Venezia on ☎041.2424 (7.30am–8pm daily), or ⊛www .hellovenezia.it or ⊛www.actv.it.
Airport enquiries Marco Polo airport, ☎041.260.9260, ⊛www.veniceairport .com.
American Express Office is located at Salizzada S. Moisè, San Marco 1471, a couple of minutes' walk west of the Piazza (Mon–Fri 9am–5.30pm, Sat 9am–12.30pm; ☎041.520.0844). Their emergency number is ☎800.64.046 (toll-free).
Banks These are concentrated on Calle Larga XXII Marzo (west of the Piazza), and along the chain of squares and alleyways between Campo S. Bartolomeo and Campo Manin (in the north of the San Marco *sestiere*). There's not much to choose between them in terms of commission and exchange rates, and their hours are generally Mon–Fri 8.30am–1.30pm and 2.30–

3.30pm. The main ones (all in San Marco) are as follows: **Banca d'Italia**, Campo S. Bartolomeo 4799; **Banca Intesa**, Calle Goldoni 4481, Calle Larga XXII Marzo 2188 & Bacino Orseolo 1126; **Banco di Roma**, Mercerie dell'Orologio 191; **Banco San Marco**, Calle Larga XXII Marzo 383.
Consulates and Embassies The **British** consulate is in Mestre at Piazzale Donatori di Sangue 2 (☎041.505.5990); this office is staffed by an honorary consul – the closest full consulate is in Milan, at Via San Paolo 7 (☎02.723.001). The nearest US consulate is also in Milan, at Via Principe Amedeo (☎02.290.351), but there's a consular office at Marco Polo airport (☎041.541.5944). Travellers from **Ireland**, **Australia**, **New Zealand** and **Canada** should contact their Rome embassies: Irish Embassy, Piazza di Campitelli 3 ☎06.697.9121; Australian Embassy, Via Alessandria 215 ☎041.06/852.721; New Zealand Embassy, Via Zara 28 ☎06.441.7171; Canadian Embassy, Via G.

B. de Rossi 27 ☎041.06/445.981.

Emergencies For police emergencies ring ☎113. Alternatively, dialling ☎112 puts you straight through to the *Carabinieri* (military police), ☎115 goes straight to the *Vigili del Fuoco* (fire brigade) and ☎118 straight to *Pronto Soccorso Medico* (ambulance).

Exchange There are clusters of exchange bureaux (*cambio*) where most tourists gather – near San Marco, the Rialto and the train station. Open late every day of the week, they can be useful in emergencies, but their rates of commission and exchange tend to be steep, with the notable exception of Travelex, which can be found at no. 142 on the Piazza, at Riva del Ferro 5126 (by the Rialto bridge) and at the airport.

Hospital Ospedale Civile, Campo SS Giovanni e Paolo ☎041.529.4111.

Internet Access Dozens of dedicated internet points have opened in the last few years; most charge €6–8 per hour, though rates usually drop the longer you stay online. Places are opening and closing all the time, but you should find the following still in operation:

San Marco: Internet Point, Campo S. Stefano 2958 (daily 10am–11pm); Venetian Navigator, Calle dei Stagneri 5239 (daily 10am–8.30pm).

Dorsoduro: Internet Point, Crosera S.Pantalon 3812a (daily 10am–11pm); Logic Internet, Calle del Traghetto 2799 (daily 10am–8.30pm).

San Polo: Network Café, Campo S. Giacomo 124, near the Rialto (Mon–Sat 10am–11pm); Venice Connection, Calle del Campanile (Mon–Sat 10am–10pm, Sun 11am–10pm).

Cannaregio: Planet Internet, Rio Terà S. Leonardo 1519 (daily 9am–11pm) by the Ponte delle Guglie; Internet Station, Sottoportego Falier 5640 (daily 10am–1pm & 3–11pm).

Castello: Internet Corner, Calle del Cafetier 6661a (Mon–Sat 10am–10pm, Sun 1–9pm); Internet Point, Calle della Sacrestia 4502 (daily 10am–11pm); Venetian

Navigator, Casselleria 5300 (daily: summer 10am–10pm; winter 10am–7.30pm) & Calle delle Bande 5269 (same hours).

Left Luggage The desk at the end of platform 14 in the train station (6am–midnight) charges €3.80 per item for five hours, then €0.60 for each of the next six hours, and €0.20 per hour thereafter. The office on Piazzale Roma (6am–9pm) charges €3.50 per item per 24hr.

Lost Property If you lose anything on the train or at the station, call ☎041.785.531; at the airport call ☎041.260.9222; on the vaporetti call ☎041.272.2179; on the buses call ☎041.272.2838; and anywhere in the city itself call ☎041.274.8225.

Police To notify police of a theft or lost passport, report to the Questura on Piazzale Roma (☎041.271.5511); in the event of an emergency, ring ☎113. There's a police station on the Piazza, at no. 63.

Post Offices Venice's main post office is in the Fondaco dei Tedeschi, near the Rialto bridge (Mon–Sat 8.30am–6.30pm). Any poste restante should be addressed to Fermo Posta, Fondaco dei Tedeschi, 80100 Venezia; take your passport when collecting your post. The principal branch post offices are in Calle dell'Ascensione, at Zàttere 1406 and by the Piazzale Roma vaporetto stops (all Mon–Sat 8.30am–6pm). Stamps can also be bought in *tabacchi*, as well as in some gift shops.

Public Toilets There are toilets on or very near to most of the main squares. You'll need a €1 coin, but the toilets are usually staffed, so you can get change; note that the Venice Card (see p.174) gives free access to many staffed toilets. The main facilities are at the train station; at Piazzale Roma; on the west side of the Accademia bridge; by the main tourist office at the Giardinetti Reali; off the west side of the Piazza; off Campo S. Bartolomeo; on Campo S. Polo; Campo Rialto Nuovo; Campo S. Leonardo; Campo San'Angelo and on Campo S. Margherita. Toilets are to be found in most of the city's bars as well; it's diplomatic, to say the least, to buy a drink before availing yourself.

Fly Less – Stay Longer!

Rough Guides believes in the good that travel does, but we are deeply aware of the impact of fuel emissions on climate change. We recommend taking fewer trips and staying for longer. If you can avoid travelling by air, please use an alternative, especially for journeys of under 1000km/600miles. And always offset your travel at ⓦ www.roughguides.com/climatechange.

Telephones Most of Venice's public call-boxes accept coins, and all of them take phone cards, which can be bought from *tabacchi* and some other shops (look for the Telecom Italia sticker), as well as from machines by the Telecom Italia phone booths in Strada Nova (near S. Felice), Piazzale Roma and adjoining the main post office building near the Rialto bridge. You're never far from a pay phone – every sizeable campo has at least one, and there are phones by most vaporetto stops. Note that many internet points offer international calls at a better rate than you'll get from Telecom Italia's public phones.

Chronology

Chronology

453 ▶ The first mass migration into the Venetian lagoon is provoked by the incursions of **Attila the Hun**'s hordes.

568 ▶ Permanent settlement is accelerated when the Germanic Lombards (or Longobards) sweep into northern Italy. The resulting confederation owes **political allegiance to Byzantium**.

726 ▶ The lagoon settlers choose their **first doge**, Orso Ipato.

810 ▶ After the Frankish army of **Charlemagne** has overrun the Lombards, the emperor's son **Pepin** sails into action against the proto-Venetians and is defeated. The lagoon settlers withdraw to the better-protected islands of **Rivoalto**, the name by which the central cluster of islands was known until the late twelfth century, when it became generally known as **Venice**.

828 ▶ With control by Byzantium little more than nominal, the Venetians signal their independence through a great symbolic act – **the theft of the body of St Mark from Alexandria**. St Mark is made the patron saint of the city in place of the Byzantine patron, St Theodore, and a basilica is built alongside the doge's castle to accommodate the holy relics. These two buildings – the **Basilica di San Marco** and the **Palazzo Ducale** – are to remain the repository of power within the city for almost one thousand years.

1000 ▶ A fleet commanded by **Doge Pietro Orseolo II** subjugates the **Slav pirates** who have been impeding Venetian trade in the northern Adriatic. The expedition is commemorated annually in the ceremony of the **Marriage of Venice to the Sea** (see p.154).

1081 ▶ The Byzantine emperor Alexius Comnenus appeals to Venice for aid against the **Normans** of southern Italy. In the following year, in a charter known as the Crisobolo (Golden Bull), the emperor declares Venetian merchants to be exempt from all tolls and taxes within his lands. In the words of one historian: "On that day Venetian world trade began."

1095 ▶ The commencement of the **First Crusade**. Offering to transport armies and supplies to the East in return for grants of property and financial bonuses, Venice extends its foothold in the Aegean, the Black Sea and Syria.

1177 ▶ Having been embroiled in the political manoeuvrings between the papacy, the Western emperor and the cities of northern Italy, Venice brings off one of its greatest diplomatic successes: **the reconciliation of Emperor Frederick Barbarossa and Pope Alexander III**.

1204 ▶ Venice plays a major role in the **Fourth Crusade** and the **Sack of Constantinople**. Thousands are massacred by the Christian soldiers and virtually every precious object that can be lifted is stolen from the city, mainly by the Venetians, who now have "one quarter and half a quarter" of the Roman Empire under their sway, with an almost uninterrupted chain of ports stretching from the lagoon to the Black Sea.

1297 ▶ The passing of the **Serrata del Maggior Consiglio**, a measure which basically allows a role in the government of the city only to those families already involved in it. The Serrata is to remain in effect, with minimal changes, until the end of the Venetian Republic five centuries later.

1310 ▶ Following an uprising led by **Bajamonte Tiepolo**, the **Council of Ten** is created to supervise internal security. Though the Council was intended to be an emergency measure, its tenure was repeatedly extended until, in 1334, it was made permanent.

1355 ▶ **Doge Marin Falier** is executed, after plotting to overthrow the councils of Venice and install himself as absolute ruler.

1380 ▶ Almost a century of sporadic warfare against Genoa – Venice's chief commercial rival in the eastern Mediterranean – climaxes with the **War of Chioggia**. The invading Genoese are driven out of the lagoon, and it soon becomes clear that Venice has at last won the tussle for economic and political supremacy.

1420 ▶ Already in control of Vicenza, Verona, Padua, Bassano, Belluno and Feltre, Venice annexes **Friuli** and **Udine**, which were formerly ruled by the King of Hungary, and thus virtually doubles the area of its *terra firma* (mainland) empire, extending it right up to the Alps.

1441 **Doge Francesco Fóscari**, having led Venice against Filippo Maria Visconti of Milan, signs the Treaty of Cremona, which confirms Venetian control of Peschiera, Brescia, Bergamo and part of the territory of Cremona.

1453 ▶ **Constantinople** falls to the Turkish army of **Sultan Mahomet II**, which results in the erosion of Venice's commercial empire in the east.

1499 ▶ The defeat of the Venetian navy at **Sapienza** leads to the loss of the main fortresses of the **Morea** (Peloponnese), which means that the Turks now control the so-called "door to the Adriatic".

1494 ▶ Italy is invaded by **Louis XII of France**. In the ensuing chaos Venice succeeds in adding bits and pieces to its *terra firma* domain, but when it begins to encroach on papal territory in Romagna, it provokes – in **1508** – the formation of the **League of Cambrai**, with Pope Julius II, Louis XII, Emperor Maximilian and the King of Spain at its head.

1516 ▶ End of the War of the League of Cambrai. Venice still possesses nearly everything it had held at the start of the war, but many of the cities of the Veneto have been sacked and the Venetian treasury bled almost dry.

1519 ▶ With the accession of the 19-year-old **Charles V**, the Habsburg Empire absorbs the massive territories of the Spanish kingdom, and the whole Italian peninsula, with the sole exception of Venice, is soon under the emperor's domination. Meanwhile, the **Turks** are on the move again – **Syria** and **Egypt** are taken in 1517; **Rhodes** falls in 1522; and by 1529 the Ottoman Empire has spread right along the southern Mediterranean to Morocco.

1571 ▶ The Venetian fleet is instrumental in the defeat of the Turks at **Lépanto**, but in subsequent negotiations Venice is forced to surrender **Cyprus**.

1606 ▶ Friction between the papacy and Venice comes to a head with a **Papal Interdict** and the excommunication of the whole city.

1669 ▶ Prolonged Turkish harassment of the Venetian colonies culminates with the fall of **Crete**.

1699 ▶ Under the command of **Doge Francesco Morosini**, the Venetians embark on a retaliatory action in the **Morea** (Peloponnese), and succeed in retaking the region, albeit for only a short time.

1718 ▶ In the **Treaty of Passarowitz** Venice is forced to accept a definition of its Mediterranean empire drawn up by the Austrians and the Turks. It is left with just the Ionian islands and the Dalmatian coast, and its power in these colonies is little more than hypothetical.

1748 ▶ By now a political nonentity, pursuing a foreign policy of unarmed neutrality, Venice signs the **Treaty of Aix-la-Chapelle**, which confirms Austrian control of what had once been Venice's mainland empire.

1797 ▶ Having mollified the Austrians by handing over the Veneto to them, **Napoleon** waits for a pretext to polish off the Republic itself. On April 20, the Venetians attack a French naval patrol off the Lido. On May 9 an ultimatum is sent to the city's government, demanding the dissolution of its constitution. On Friday, **May 12, 1797** the Maggior Consiglio (in effect the city's parliament) meets for the last time, voting to accede to Napoleon's demands. The Venetian Republic is dead. By the **Treaty of Campo Formio**, signed in October, Napoleon relinquishes Venice to the Austrians.

1805 ▶ Napoleon joins the city to his Kingdom of Italy, and it stays **under French domination** until the aftermath of Waterloo.

1815 ▶ Venice passes back to the **Austrians** again, and remains a Habsburg province for the next half-century, the only break in Austrian rule coming with the **revolt of March 1848**, when the city is reinstituted as a republic under the leadership of **Daniele Manin**. The rebellion lasts until August 1849.

1866 ▶ Venice is absorbed into the Kingdom of United Italy.

1869 ▶ The opening of the Suez Canal brings a muted revival to the shipbuilders of Venice's Arsenale, but **tourism** is now emerging as the main area of economic expansion, with the development of the **Lido** as Europe's most fashionable resort.

1917 ▶ The Italian navy dismantles the Arsenale and switches its yards to Genoa and Naples.

1933 ▶ A **road link** is built to carry workers between Venice and the steadily expanding refineries and factories of **Porto**

Marghera. Rapid depopulation of the historic centre soon follows, as workers decamp to Marghera's neighbour, **Mestre**, where housing is drier, roomier, warmer and cheaper to maintain than apartments in Venice. (The population of Mestre-Marghera is today more than three times that of the historic centre of Venice, which is around the 62,000 mark and falling by around 1500 with each passing year. Immediately after World War II it was around 170,000.)

1989 ▶ By now, tourism is generating almost seventy percent of the city's income, and as many as fifteen million tourists are coming to Venice each year. On so-called "Black Sunday", July 15, 1989, the figure hits 150,000 for a single day.

2003 ▶ With the number of annual *aque alte* (floods) exceeding a hundred, in April work begins on the construction of the tidal barrier (see p.153).

Language

The basics

What follows is a brief pronunciation guide and a run-down of essential words and phrases. For more detail, get *Italian: Rough Guide Phrasebook*, which has a huge but accessible vocabulary in dictionary format, a grammar section, a detailed menu reader and useful scenarios. These scenarios can also be downloaded free as audio files from Ⓦ www.roughguides.com.

Pronunciation

Italian **pronunciation** is easy, since every word is spoken exactly as it is written. The only difficulties you are likely to encounter are the few **consonants** that are different from English:

c before e or i is pronounced as in **ch**urch, while **ch** before the same vowels is hard, as in **c**at.

sci or **sce** are pronounced as in **sh**eet and **sh**elter respectively.

g is soft before **e** and **i**, as in **g**eranium; hard when followed by **h**, as in **g**arlic.

gn has the ni sound of our "o**ni**on".

gl in Italian is softened to something like li in English, as in stal**li**on.

h is not aspirated, as in **h**onour.

All Italian words are **stressed** on the penultimate syllable unless an **accent** (´ or `) denotes otherwise, although written accents are often left out in practice. Note that the ending **–ia** or **–ie** counts as two syllables, hence *trattoria* is stressed on the **i**.

Words and phrases

Basic words and phrases

Good morning	Buon giorno	I don't know	Non lo so
Good afternoon/ evening	Buona sera	Excuse me	Mi scusi/Prego
		Excuse me (in a crowd)	Permesso
Good night	Buona notte	I'm sorry	Mi dispiace
Goodbye	Arrivederci	I'm English	Sono inglese
Yes	Sì	Scottish	scozzese
No	No	American	americano
Please	Per favore	Irish	irlandese
Thank you (very much)	Grázie (molte/mille grazie)	Welsh	gallese
		Today	Oggi
		Tomorrow	Domani
You're welcome	Prego	Day after tomorrow	Dopodomani
Alright/that's OK	Va bene	Yesterday	Ieri
How are you?	Come stai/sta? (informal/formal)	Now	Adesso
		Later	Più tardi
		Wait a minute!	Aspetta!
I'm fine	Bene	In the morning	Di mattina
Do you speak English?	Parla inglese?	In the afternoon	Nel pomeriggio
		In the evening	Di sera
I don't understand	Non ho capito	Here/there	Qui/La

LANGUAGE

The basics

Good/bad	Buono/Cattivo
Big/small	Grande/Píccoo
Cheap/expensive	Económico/Caro
Hot/cold	Caldo/Freddo
Near/far	Vicino/Lontano
Vacant/occupied	Libero/Occupato
With/without	Con/Senza
More/less	Più/Meno
Enough, no more	Basta
Mr . . .	Signor . . .
Mrs . . .	Signora . . .
Miss . . .	Signorina . . .

(il Signor, la Signora, la Signorina when speaking about someone else)

Numbers

1	uno
2	due
3	tre
4	quattro
5	cinque
6	sei
7	sette
8	otto
9	nove
10	dieci
11	undici
12	dodici
13	tredici
14	quattordici
15	quindici
16	sedici
17	diciassette
18	diciotto
19	diciannove
20	venti
21	ventuno
22	ventidue
30	trenta
40	quaranta
50	cinquanta
60	sessanta
70	settanta
80	ottanta
90	novanta
100	cento
101	centuno
110	centodieci
200	duecento
500	cinquecento
1000	mille
5000	cinquemila
10,000	diecimila
50,000	cinquantamila

Some signs

Entrance/exit	Entrata/Uscita
Open/closed	Aperto/Chiuso
Arrivals/ departures	Arrivi/Partenze
Closed for restoration	Chiuso per restauro
Closed for holidays	Chiuso per ferie
Pull/push	Tirare/Spingere
Do not touch	Non toccare
Danger	Perícolo
Beware	Attenzione
First aid	Pronto soccorso
Ring the bell	Suonare il campanello
No smoking	Vietato fumare

Transport

Ferry	Traghetto
Bus station	Autostazione
Train station	Stazione ferroviaria
A ticket to . . .	Un biglietto a . . .
One-way/return	Solo andata/ andata e ritorno
What time does it leave?	A che ora parte?
Where does it leave from?	Da dove parte?

Accommodation

Hotel	Albergo
Do you have a room . . .	Ha una cámera . . .
for one/two/three people	per una/due/tre person(a/e)
for one/two/three nights	per una/due/tre nott(e/i)
for one/two weeks	per una/due settiman(a/e)
with a double bed	con un letto matrimoniale
with a shower/ bath	con una doccia/ un bagno
How much is it?	Quanto costa?
Is breakfast included?	È compresa la prima colazione?
Do you have anything cheaper?	Ha niente che costa di meno?
I'll take it	La prendo
I'd like to book a room	Vorrei prenotare una cámera

I have a booking	Ho una prenotazione
Youth hostel	Ostello per la gioventù

In the restaurant

A table	Una tavola
I'd like to book a table for two people at eight o'clock	Vorrei prenotare una tavola per due alle quattro
We need a knife	Abbiamo bisogno di un coltello
a fork	una forchetta
a spoon	un cucchiaio
a glass	un bicchiere
What do you recommend?	Che cosa mi consiglia lei?
Waiter/waitress!	Cameriere/a!
Bill/check	Il conto
Is service included	È incluso il servizio?
I'm a vegetarian	Sono vegetariano/a

Questions and directions

Where?	Dove?
(where is/are . . ?)	(Dov'è/Dove sono)
When?	Quando?
What? (what is it?)	Cosa? (Cos'è?)
How much/many?	Quanto/Quanti?
Why?	Perché?
It is/there is	È/C'è
(is it/is there . . ?)	(È/C'è . . . ?)
What time is it?	Che ora è/ Che ore sono?
How do I get to . . ?	Come arrivo a . . ?
What time does it open?	A che ora apre?
What time does it close?	A che ora chiude?
How much does it cost ?	Quanto costa?
(. . do they cost?)	(Quanto cóstano?)
What's it called in Italian?	Come si chiama in italiano?

Menu reader

This glossary should allow you to decode most menus; it concludes with a summary of Venetian specialities.

Basics and snacks

Aceto	Vinegar
Aglio	Garlic
Biscotti	Biscuits
Burro	Butter
Caramelle	Sweets
Cioccolato	Chocolate
Focaccia	Oven-baked bread-based snack
Formaggio	Cheese
Frittata	Omelette
Gelato	Ice cream
Grissini	Bread sticks
Marmellata	Jam
Olio	Oil
Olive	Olives
Pane	Bread
Pane integrale	Wholemeal bread
Panino	Bread roll
Patatine	Crisps
Patatine fritte	Chips
Pepe	Pepper
Pizzetta	Small cheese-and-tomato pizza
Riso	Rice
Sale	Salt
Tramezzini	Sandwich
Uova	Eggs
Yogurt	Yoghurt
Zúcchero	Sugar
Zuppa	Soup

Starters (antipasti)

Antipasto misto	Mixed cold meats and cheese (and a selection of other things in this list)
Caponata	Mixed aubergine, olives, tomatoes and celery
Caprese	Tomato and mozzarella salad
Insalata di mare	Seafood salad
Insalata di riso	Rice salad
Melanzane in parmigiana	Fried aubergine in tomato and parmesan cheese

Mortadella	Salami-type cured meat
Pancetta	Bacon
Peperonata	Grilled green, red or yellow peppers stewed in olive oil
Pomodori ripieni	Stuffed tomatoes
Prosciutto	Ham
Salame	Salami

Soups

Brodo	Clear broth
Minestrina	Any light soup
Minestrone	Thick vegetable soup
Pasta e fagioli	Pasta soup with beans
Pastina in brodo	Pasta pieces in clear broth
Stracciatella	Broth with egg

Pasta

Cannelloni	Large tubes of pasta, stuffed
Farfalle	Literally "bow"-shaped pasta; the word also means "butterflies"
Fettuccine	Narrow pasta ribbons
Gnocchi	Small potato and dough dumplings
Lasagne	Lasagne
Maccheroni	Tubular spaghetti
Pasta al forno	Pasta baked with minced meat, eggs, tomato and cheese
Penne	Smaller version of rigatoni
Ravioli	Small packets of stuffed pasta
Rigatoni	Large, grooved tubular pasta
Risotto	Cooked rice dish, with sauce
Spaghetti	Spaghetti
Spaghettini	Thin spaghetti
Tagliatelle	Pasta ribbons, another word for fettuccine
Tortellini	Small rings of pasta, stuffed with meat or cheese
Vermicelli	Very thin spaghetti (literally "little worms")

Pasta sauces

Aglio e olio	Tossed in garlic and olive oil
(e peperoncino)	(and hot chillies)
Arrabbiata	Spicy tomato sauce
Bolognese	Meat sauce
Burro e salvia	Butter and sage
Carbonara	Cream, ham and beaten egg
Frutta di mare	Seafood
Funghi	Mushroom
Matriciana	Cubed pork and tomato sauce
Panna	Cream
Parmigiano	Parmesan cheese
Pesto	Ground basil, pine nut, garlic and pecorino sauce
Pomodoro	Tomato sauce
Ragù	Meat sauce
Vóngole	Clam and tomato sauce

Meat (carne)

Agnello	Lamb
Bistecca	Steak
Coniglio	Rabbit
Costolette	Chops
Cotolette	Cutlets
Fegatini	Chicken livers
Fégato	Liver
Involtini	Steak slices, rolled and stuffed
Lingua	Tongue
Maiale	Pork
Manzo	Beef
Ossobuco	Shin of veal
Pollo	Chicken
Polpette	Meatballs (or balls of anything minced)
Rognoni	Kidneys
Salsiccia	Sausage
Saltimbocca	Veal with ham
Spezzatino	Stew
Tacchino	Turkey
Trippa	Tripe
Vitello	Veal

Fish (pesce) and shellfish (crostacei)

Acciughe	Anchovies
Anguilla	Eel
Aragosta	Lobster
Baccalà	Dried salted cod
Bronzino/ Branzino	Sea-bass

Calamari	Squid
Cape lungue	Razor clams
Cape sante	Scallops
Caparossoli	Shrimps
Coda di rospo	Monkfish
Cozze	Mussels
Dentice	Dentex (like sea-bass)
Gamberetti	Shrimps
Gámberi	Prawns
Granchio	Crab
Merluzzo	Cod
Orata	Bream
Ostriche	Oysters
Pescespada	Swordfish
Pólipo	Octopus
Ricci di mare	Sea urchins
Rombo	Turbot
San Pietro	John Dory
Sarde	Sardines
Schie	Shrimps
Seppie	Cuttlefish
Sógliola	Sole
Tonno	Tuna
Triglie	Red mullet
Trota	Trout
Vóngole	Clams

Vegetables (contorni) and salad (insalata)

Asparagi	Asparagus
Basílico	Basil
Bróccoli	Broccoli
Cápperi	Capers
Carciofi	Artichokes
Carciofini	Artichoke hearts
Carotte	Carrots
Cavolfiori	Cauliflower
Cávolo	Cabbage
Ceci	Chickpeas
Cetriolo	Cucumber
Cipolla	Onion
Fagioli	Beans
Fagiolini	Green beans
Finocchio	Fennel
Funghi	Mushrooms
Insalata verde/ insalata mista	Green salad/ mixed salad
Melanzana	Aubergine/eggplant
Orígano	Oregano
Patate	Potatoes
Peperoni	Peppers
Piselli	Peas
Pomodori	Tomatoes
Radicchio	Chicory
Spinaci	Spinach

| Zucchini | Courgettes |
| Zucca | Pumpkin |

Desserts (dolci)

Amaretti	Macaroons
Cassata	Ice-cream cake with candied fruit
Gelato	Ice cream
Macedonia	Fruit salad
Torta	Cake, tart
Zabaglione	Dessert made with eggs, sugar and Marsala wine
Zuppa Inglese	Trifle

Cheese (formaggi)

Caciocavallo	A type of dried, mature mozzarella cheese
Fontina	Northern Italian cheese used in cooking
Gorgonzola	Soft blue-veined cheese
Mozzarella	Bland soft white cheese used on pizzas
Parmigiano	Parmesan cheese
Pecorino	Strong-tasting hard sheep's cheese
Provolone	Hard strong cheese
Ricotta	Soft white cheese made from ewe's milk, used in sweet or savoury dishes

Fruit (frutta) and nuts (noce)

Ananas	Pineapple
Anguria/ Coccómero	Watermelon
Arance	Oranges
Banane	Bananas
Ciliege	Cherries
Fichi	Figs
Fichi d'India	Prickly pears
Frágole	Strawberries
Limone	Lemon
Mándorle	Almonds
Mele	Apples
Melone	Melon
Pere	Pears
Pesche	Peaches

Pignoli	Pine nuts
Pistacchio	Pistachio nut
Uva	Grapes

Drinks (bevande)

Acqua minerale	Mineral water
Aranciata	Orangeade
Bicchiere	Glass
Birra	Beer
Bottiglia	Bottle
Caffè	Coffee
Cioccolata calda	Hot chocolate
Ghiaccio	Ice
Granita	Iced coffee or fruit drink
Latte	Milk
Limonata	Lemonade

Selz	Soda water
Spremuta	Fresh fruit juice
Spumante	Sparkling wine
Succo	Concentrated fruit juice with sugar
Tè	Tea
Tónico	Tonic water
Vino	Wine
Rosso	Red
Bianco	White
Rosato	Rosé
Secco	Dry
Dolce	Sweet
Litro	Litre
Mezzo	Half
Quarto	Quarter
Salute!	Cheers!

Venetian specialities

Antipasti (starters) e Primi (first course)

Acciughe marinate	Marinated anchovies with onions
Bigoli in salsa	Spaghetti with butter, onions and sardines
Brodetto	Mixed fish soup, often with tomatoes and garlic
Castraura	Artichoke hearts
Granseola alla Veneziana	Crab cooked with oil, parsley and lemon
Pasta e fagioli	Pasta and beans
San Prosciutto Daniele	The best-quality prosciutto
Risotto di mare	Mixed seafood risotto
Risotto di cape	Risotto with clams and shellfish
Risotto alla sbirraglia	Risotto with chicken, vegetables and ham
Risotto alla trevigiana	Risotto with butter, onions and chicory
Sopa de peoci	Mussel soup with garlic and parsley

Secondi (second course)

Anguilla alla Veneziana	Eel cooked with lemon and tuna
Baccalà mantecato	Salt cod simmered in milk
Fegato veneziana	Sliced calf's liver cooked in olive oil with onion
Peoci salati	Mussels with parsley and garlic
Risi e bisi	Rice and peas, with parmesan and ham
Sarde in saor	Marinated sardines
Seppie in nero	Squid cooked in its ink
Seppioline nere	Baby cuttlefish cooked in its ink

Dolci

Frittole alla Veneziana	Rum- and anise-flavoured fritters filled with pine nuts, raisins and candied fruit
Tiramisù	Dessert of layered chocolate and cream, flavoured with rum and coffee

- **Read** Rough Guides' trusted travel info

- **Access** exclusive articles from Rough Guides authors

- **Update** yourself on new books, maps, CDs and other products

- **Enter** our competitions and win travel prizes

- **Share** ideas, journals, photos & travel advice with other users

- **Earn** points every time you contribute to the Rough Guide
  community and get rewards

BROADEN YOUR HORIZONS

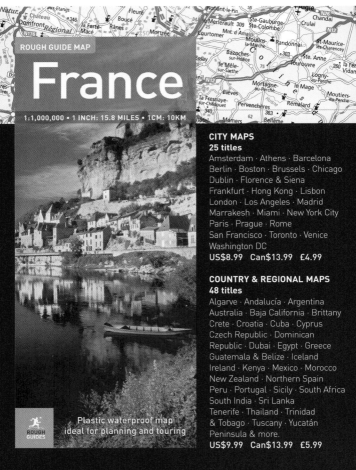

small print & Index

A Rough Guide to Rough Guides

In 1981, Mark Ellingham, a recent graduate in English from Bristol University, was travelling in Greece on a tiny budget and couldn't find the right guidebook. With a group of friends he wrote his own guide, combining a contemporary, journalistic style with a practical approach to travellers' needs. That first Rough Guide was a student scheme that became a publishing phenomenon. Today, Rough Guides include recommendations from shoestring to luxury and cover hundreds of destinations around the globe, including almost every country in the Americas and Europe, more than half of Africa and most of Asia and Australasia. Millions of readers relish Rough Guides' wit and inquisitiveness as much as their enthusiastic, critical approach and value-for-money ethos. The guides' ever-growing team of authors and photographers is spread all over the world.

In the early 1990s, Rough Guides branched out of travel, with the publication of Rough Guides to World Music, Classical Music and the Internet. All three have become benchmark titles in their fields, spearheading the publication of a range of more than 350 titles under the Rough Guide name, including phrasebooks, waterproof maps, music guides from Opera to Heavy Metal, reference works as diverse as Conspiracy Theories and Shakespeare, and popular culture books from iPods to Poker. Rough Guides also produce a series of more than 120 World Music CDs in partnership with World Music Network.

Visit www.roughguides.com to see our latest publications.

Rough Guide travel images are available for commercial licensing at www.roughguidespictures.com

Publishing information

This second edition published March 2007 by Rough Guides Ltd, 80 Strand, London WC2R 0RL; 345 Hudson St, 4th Floor, New York, NY 10014, USA.

Distributed by the Penguin Group
Penguin Books Ltd, 80 Strand, London WC2R 0RL
Penguin Group (USA), 375 Hudson St, NY 10014, USA
14 Local Shopping Centre, Panchsheel Park, New Delhi 110017, India
Penguin Group (Australia), 250 Camberwell Rd, Camberwell, Victoria 3124, Australia
Penguin Group (Canada), 10 Alcorn Ave, Toronto, ON M4V 1E4, Canada
Penguin Group (NZ), 67 Apollo Drive, Mairangi Bay, Auckland 1310, New Zealand

Typeset in Bembo and Helvetica to an original design by Henry Iles.

Cover concept by Peter Dyer

Printed and bound in China

208pp includes index

A catalogue record for this book is available from the British Library

ISBN 13: 978-1-84353-757-1

Help us update

We've gone to a lot of effort to ensure that the second edition of Venice DIRECTIONS is accurate and up- to- date. However, things change – places get "discovered", opening hours are notoriously fickle, restaurants and rooms raise prices or lower standards. If you feel we've got it wrong or left something out, we'd like to know, and if you can remember the address, the price, the phone number, so much the better.

We'll credit all contributions, and send a copy of the next edition (or any other DIRECTIONS guide or Rough Guide if you prefer) for the best letters. Everyone who writes to us and isn't already a subscriber will receive a copy of our full-colour thrice-yearly newsletter. Please mark letters: "Venice DIRECTIONS Update" and send to: Rough Guides, 80 Strand, London WC2R 0RL, or Rough Guides, 4th Floor, 345 Hudson St, New York, NY 10014. Or send an email to mail@roughguides.com

Have your questions answered and tell others about your trip at www.roughguides.atinfopop.com

Rough Guide credits

Text editor: Karoline Densley
Layout: Umesh Aggarwal
Photography: James McConnachie
Cartography: Karobi Gogoi

Picture editor: Alex Myers
Proofreader: Jennifer Speake
Production: Aimee Hampson
Cover design: Chlöe Roberts

SMALL PRINT

The author

Jonathan Buckley writes the *Rough Guide to Venice*, is the co-author of *Rough Guides* to Tuscany & Umbria and Florence, and has published five novels: *The Biography of Thomas Lang, Xerxes, Ghost MacIndoe, Invisible* and *So He Takes the Dog*.

Readers' letter

Philip Ainsworth, Edward Bacon, Roger Bowder, Jean-Luc Breton, Mandi Brooker, John Brooks, Pam Cantle, Roger Carruthers, Brian Cooney, Charles Daly, Ann Feltham, Dave Gilmour, Bettina Hartas, Kurt & Catherine Kullmann, Sophia Lambert, Ray Massey, Danielle Neville, Mary-Elizabeth Raw, Andrew Sides, Geoff Taylor, Graham Thomas, Christen K. Thomsen, Jeanne Tift.

Index

Maps are marked in colour